About the Author

Girl Gone Greek is Rebecca Hall's debut Contemporary Women's Fiction Novel. After extensive global travels, Rebecca left the UK to return to the country she fell in love with—Greece, where she teaches English, writes and wryly observes that the chaotic nature of her adopted country actually suits her personality very well. All travel experiences, & particularly living in versatile cultures, have helped to shape who she is today. She is a *Rough Guide* co-author *(Greece* and *The Greek Islands)* and has contributed to numerous publications including *Apollo Business Class Magazine* for *Cyprus Airways* and *Let's Go* for *RyanAir*, the *Daily Telegraph* Travel Section and her container ship voyage from Athens to Hong Kong caught the eye of *NPR National Radio* in the United States, where she was interviewed twice. When not writing, you'll usually find her drinking coffee with her friends, or sourcing a new place to eat baklava. Follow her adventures at:

www.lifebeyondbordersblog.com
www.facebook.com/LifeBeyondBordersBlog
www.twitter.com/BeyondBex
www.instagram.com/BeyondBex

ATHENS - AUG 16

TO/ David and family,

Thank you so much for supporting
'Girl Gone Greek.'

I hope our paths cross one day.

Kind regards,

Rebecca
Hall

GIRL

GONE

GREEK

by

Rebecca

A

Hall

Author's Note/Disclaimer

This book is a combination of facts and embellishment
about a period of my life in Greece. While the events are
based on fact, some names and identifying details have
been changed to protect the privacy of those involved,
and some parts have been semi-fictionalized to varying
degrees for various purposes.

Copyright

Editor: Perry Iles
Artist: Simon Avery
Interior Book Design: Natascha Maria

Printed by CreateSpace
Available in paperback and Kindle versions
First Printing 2015, ISBN 978-1512251883

For my dad

GIRL GONE GREEK

Summer

Chapter 1

I gazed at the wall, gritting my teeth. My sister Kirsty was in town on a visit.

"Let's face it Rachel," she said, "being the youngest you always did have to be that bit different. At least I've had children and secured a serious job." She tapped me on the knee, "Mark my words, I've got ten years on you, and the way you're carrying on is unsustainable." She settled back in her chair with a smug grin.

"Don't forget you've got a divorce now, too," I shrugged, dipping a Digestive into my tea. We'd never really seen eye-to-eye, my sister and me.

"Well, you managed to last out a whole degree course in your thirties," Kirsty said. She got up and strolled across the kitchen to switch on the kettle, either failing to hear or choosing to ignore my comment, "and we never thought you'd finish that, just like so many of your other fanciful ideas. I guess why not do a TEFL course?" She shook her head, "It's just the sort of thing you *would* do."

I exchanged a look with Dad, who was busy preparing dinner for us. Even in his 70s, he loved to try new things, and cooking was one of them.

"It would be nice if you could offer some support instead of finding fault all the time," I suggested. "You've

always been the naysayer of this family, Kirsty, especially when it comes to me."

Leaning against the kitchen counter, she smirked.
"Ha! Well, what do you expect, Rachel? You were
the only one to fail your Eleven Plus exam at primary
school. Looking back, that should've been an indication
of how you'd continue through life. And what about the
time you were one of two people in your class, out of
how many—thirty, wasn't it?—to get the lowest grade
in your Maths GCSE. Is it any wonder I can't take you
seriously?"

"I volunteered with young kids in Sri Lanka and
Cambodia," I hated myself at that moment for allowing
her to drag me to the point where I felt like I had to make
excuses for myself. I could either rise to her bait and
start an argument, or respond with dignity and grace and
say nothing. I chose the latter option...but felt like I was
grinding my teeth to a fine powder. I kept the visions of
sororicide to myself.

Kirsty clearly had a certain view of TEFL teachers,
and the double whammy was that one of them was now
going to be her younger sister.

Is she jealous? Her long brown hair looks particu-
larly greasy today and judging by the way she's wolfing
down those chocolate biscuits, the Atkins Diet isn't
working out. I reached over and took another biscuit,
fleetingly smiling at the fact that I could eat them to my
heart's content without having to strike up a relationship
with Mr. Atkins might not help sibling bonding.

"You just love being the Little Miss Victim of this
family—assuming no-one loves you," said Kirsty.

You think? With a sister like you, is that any

surprise? I tried to tune her incessant nagging out, humming women-empowering Aretha Franklin tunes in my head—*R E S P E C T-Find out what it means to me.*

"Besides," Kirsty continued, "how hard, really, can a one-month TEFL course be? It's not like it'll lead to a proper career, unlike my teaching degree. You'll bum around for a few years like those other TEFL hippies. Never saw you as the Jesus-sandal-wearing type, always thought you saw yourself as above all that."

"Dad, can't you say something to her?" I pleaded, once again hating myself more than anything for the fact I allowed myself to feel—and act—like a three year old in my older sister's company.

"Not fair for me to get involved sweetheart." Dad, as much as I loved him, was quite a weak man when it came to family emotions and took the usual male route of avoiding conflict where and when possible. He offered a sympathetic smile and turned back to concentrating on the task of peeling potatoes.

So, holding my breath, lest I say something I'd regret, I kissed him on the cheek before bolting for the door. I needed fresh air, fast. I ignored Kirsty's barbs and tried to focus on the positive; at least on one point we actually agreed with each other, even if she was being malicious: how hard, really, could a TEFL course be?

What's everyone thinking? We sat in the classroom, ten strangers who were due to take up a whole new set of challenges and responsibilities for a month. I'd chosen to study in Cornwall. *(It's only an hour and*

11

a half's drive each way...I can be home before it gets dark.) This is an ideal place to study, I reassured myself, growing increasingly nervous as the silence dragged on. *Jeez, when's this going to start?*

Gloria, the trainer, swept into the room some ten minutes late, just as the quiet was becoming deafening, and after polite introductions broke it to us:

"You will be teaching from tomorrow. You'll be expected to undertake five written assignments over the duration of this course, the first to be handed in by the end of this week. That's right, this Friday. You must plan for the lessons you teach and show them to me for approval before you teach them."

A young man who looked to be in his twenties shot up his hand.

"So if we're teaching tomorrow, we'll need to plan a lesson tonight and hand it to you tomorrow morning?" He looked as panicked as I felt.

"That's right," beamed Gloria. "But you're all intelligent people, you'll cope."

I looked around at the sea of equally shell-shocked faces. A small part of me had half-agreed with Ugly Big Sister that TEFL would merely be an opportunity to bum around a bit before making up my mind when to settle down and get a career; it'd be easy. But I had no intention of letting Kirsty know this, and taking the workload into consideration I quickly realised my three hour round-commute would be too much to bear. I decided that from tomorrow I'd find somewhere local to stay. Anyway, it might be pleasant to stay in Cornwall for a month over the summer. I envisaged myself lounging on the beach at the weekends. They couldn't expect us to work non-stop, could they? But judging by Gloria's announcement about daily teaching slots and weekly assignments, it appeared that the trainers did, in fact, expect us to do just that.

So, with my visions of learning to surf on the beaches of North Cornwall banished I found a flat with two fellow course-mates...above the local tropical fish shop. Unfortunately, the gurgle of all the fish tanks at night prevented anything approaching a good night's sleep, but the three of us supported each other well throughout our month of hell. Calling it hell was no exaggeration—it was harder than all three years of university put together. It was only when I started to get very, very tearful because I couldn't remember the difference between present perfect and present continuous verbs that my fellow flatmates, Tom and Sandra, took me under their collective wing and dragged me away from my current lesson planning.

"OK Rachel, time out. We're having a night off and going to the cinema," insisted Sandra. "You *will* come with us. Get out of your pyjamas, get dressed, brush that mop on your head and stop looking like a local." Sandra clearly didn't rate the Cornish population very highly, and I had to admit I'd seen a few people wandering around the town looking frighteningly vacant—similar to my current state. My appearance, however, was study-induced and not a by-product of the shallowness of my gene pool.

"But I have to teach the German teens tomorrow, and they'll eat me alive if I don't get this lesson right... their grammar knowledge is better than mine! Can't you see their smirks in class?" I paced around the room, chewing my thumbnail.

"I don't care, it'll do you good," said Tom, prising the textbook from my hands and throwing it onto the couch. "Besides, you'll love this movie, it's a sing-along version of *Mamma Mia*."

I made my way to the hallway mirror to comb my hair. A mental health night was just what the doctor ordered; it'd refresh and revitalise me. Refusing to give up, I'd show Kirsty; English grammar hadn't beaten me yet.

We jumped into Sandra's car and headed into town for some well-deserved entertainment.

I met my reflection in the mirror as I got ready for bed after *Mamma Mia*, and a knowing grin crossed my face. *I can do it: find my paradise in Greece after TEFL.*

I have a habit of labelling things, especially significant events that shape my life. The *Mamma Mia* evening was one such event. It helped me realise where I'd apply to go for my first English teaching job when I finished this course from hell.

I'd visited various places around the globe, and the farther they were from home the better I liked them…a psychological side effect of the negative relationship I had with my sister. I always held the belief that there *must* be something unlikeable about me, due to Kirsty's relentless animosity, so Greece would give me a chance to re-invent myself and be liked by others. Initially I'd intended to teach in a far-flung destination: Vietnam, maybe. My surface motivation for this was sunshine, swimming and a complete change of culture. When you're conditioned to the wet, grey weather of the UK, the chance of a job in a different climate and country—a new life and new friends who accept you with no interest in who you were, but what you are—is certainly appealing. At first I'd thought anything in Europe was too near—both geographically and culturally. But there were things I wasn't so eager to run away from (yes, I had a vague notion I might be running, but was prepared to). My Dad, for example. He'd never ask me to stay, but he was getting older. If something happened I wanted to be near enough to come at a moment's notice. But why not go to Spain? If it was sunshine and swimming I was after, I could go to any Mediterranean country.

The final push in the internal compass that pointed me towards Greece was the memories *Mamma Mia* stirred up. I remembered happier family times, holidays there when I was younger; blue skies, whitewashed houses and a laid back attitude to life. Dad had once had business contacts in Greece and would chuckle as he reminisced on his time there; "They refuse to wear seatbelts in their cars or crash helmets on their bikes, even though it's for their own safety. It's because it's a law, because they're being told what to do. You know how to get a Greek to obey the speed limit? Put a sign on the national road that says 'Do not, under any circumstances, drive at 70km an hour' and they'll do it, purely because they've been told not to," he'd joke. I liked the idea of living in a slightly anarchical society…a place where authority was looked down upon. Unconventional from birth and always in trouble for questioning too much at school, I figured if I was going to make an "awful life-plan," I might as well make it in a country that would more readily understand this character trait of mine.

In the meantime I had a lot to do: find a job, rent my property in the UK, promise Dad I wouldn't meet— and run off with—some Onassis-type *(although the money would be nice, I mused to myself)*. Dad had always been protective of me, probably because I was by far his youngest and while he never said much, he was mindful of the scorn Kirsty heaped on me. This protectiveness had mutated into the realm of believing that no man was good enough for his daughter. "And especially not a Greek man," he had once said, based on his intimate knowledge of Greeks and their character traits. "They're all mummy's boys…you'll always be second."

My flatmates and I had undertaken the all-important task of holding the 'End of TEFL Hell' party. Taking a moment to ourselves in the kitchen, we pondered our post-TEFL futures that had taken a back seat during the last days of our course.

"Why Greece, Rachel?" Brian asked, leaning against the kitchen counter.

"She doesn't want to join me in Japan, that's why" called Richard from the sitting room, leaning over the arm of the sofa to throw a wink at me. Although Richard already had two years' experience teaching in Japan, he'd been just as shell-shocked as I was on our first day. Due to his experience, he was the first one we'd all turned to when the verbs became too much, and he'd supported us all really well.

"Yeah, I'm sure she'll give up her life plans for a man she's only known for one month," said Sandra, pointing a carrot stick at him.

"Huh! People give up more after 'knowing' someone for one night" Richard became defensive. I smiled at him, replying "I'm sure my sister wouldn't be surprised if I did hop on a plane to Japan with you. I do, after all, lead an 'irresponsible life.'"

"You naughty rolling stone, Rachel" Sandra slapped me on the wrist. "Don't you listen to anyone else. Just follow your gut instinct. Family can be full of good intentions, but they interfere too much—I should know," she sighed, a slightly glazed look coming over her.

Sandra was in her early thirties and about to head off to Finland to live with her new boyfriend (who she'd known for longer than one month). She was planning to teach English while she was there and from our conversations, it was clear her parents didn't approve of her nomadic lifestyle and wanted her to settle down in the UK and provide them with grandchildren. It was nice to speak to someone who understood what it was like to have people criticise and disapprove of the way you lived, people who were supposed to be supportive. Blood ties weren't guarantees of a great relationship and I felt lucky to have shared a flat with both her and Tom for one month, the intensity of the course and our similar backgrounds bonding us.

I turned back to Brian. "I loved Asia when I was there and I certainly do like the idea of going further than Europe, but there's something that draws me to Greece.

I need to go and discover the real country and culture, not just what the tourists see, I need to be in a place that supports this anti-authoritarian side of me. What about you? Where'll you go?"

He seemed less enthusiastic about his TEFL future. "They need someone who's TEFL qualified at my school here in deepest, darkest Cornwall. Winking he added "I might come and visit you in the land of *Mamma Mia*, as well as Rich in Japan...or Sandra in Finland. Who knows? I've got the whole world to choose from now, after meeting you fine people." He motioned to the party in the next room.

Brian was right—even though from different backgrounds, we all shared a passion to experience and understand different cultures, and we'd seen TEFL as a route to doing this. My other flatmate Tom didn't really know what he was going to do with his qualification, but just felt it'd help him with his primary school career. Like Brian, schools were starting to see the need to have TEFL qualified teachers.

"Cheers everyone!" I raised my glass just as *Dancing Queen* came through the iPod, and I smiled once again, knowing soon I would be winging my way to Greece.

Chapter 2

Arriving at Gatwick Airport, I fought tears as I hugged Dad goodbye. The gate for my easyjet flight to Athens had been announced, and now, after at least a week of packing, unpacking, re-packing and wondering if the Tetley teabags and Robinsons Orange Barley Water were *really* necessary (they were), I was heading to Athens after paying an excess baggage fee of £75. Why did airlines insist on punishing people who were brave enough to change their lives, yet still needed the occasional home comfort? It seemed it wasn't only Kirsty who disapproved of my life plan.

Dad insisted on driving me to the airport, and was mildly OCD about not wanting to be late. The weather had been characteristically miserable on the drive up: dark clouds and drizzly rain. We'd arrived two hours before check-in had even opened, forcing us to make small talk...neither one acknowledging the massive elephant trumpeting away in the departure lounge—the fact that I was leaving and we'd have to say goodbye.

My family isn't particularly expressive. I knew that despite all his moaning about getting a backache during the long drive, Dad had taken me so that he could do as much for me as he possibly could—right up to the last minute. This even included arranging a hotel for my first night in Athens.

At last, the PA announced the final call. I really had to go.

"It's only Greece, Dad. It's not like I'm off to the South Pacific again, or that village in Sri Lanka," (I'd kept the Love Match offers during my three month teaching stint there to myself). "And I know I'm your youngest, but I'm not *young* anymore."

But I seemed to be reassuring myself more than him; despite all his help and company, he looked less upset about me leaving this time. In fact, he had a look of affection that I suspected went further than his feelings for me.

"It's Greece," he said, as he caught my inquisitive stare. "You'll see what I mean when you get there. I'm convinced that this trip will finally cure you of your dromomania."

"My *what*?" I contemplated—not for the first time—the irony that it was Dad who was a walking dictionary, whilst I was the one who intended to be an English teacher.

"Look it up on that Googly thing you're always using these days, see if I'm not right. Now go and get that plane, I don't want to have driven here two hours early—and get a bad back to boot—only for you to miss it." I smiled inwardly...he still had to get his moan in there somehow.

"I love you, Dad." He enveloped me in an awkward bear hug—despite checking in a huge bag, I still had an inordinate amount of hand-luggage too—pinched my cheek in a Greek manner and then backed away towards the exit, smiling. The fact he seemed relaxed about me leaving made me feel more excited and less nervous. I waved as I took myself, teabags and all, through to the Passengers Only departure area that heralded the first part of my adventure.

"Please return to your seats, ladies and gentlemen. Restore your tables and seats to their upright and locked positions. We will be commencing our final approach into Athens in ten minutes," the stewardess announced over the intercom. I obeyed, looking out through the window into a cloudless evening, and I recalled an earlier announcement stating that the temperature in Athens, although September, was still a balmy twenty-five degrees…a far cry from the drizzly grey weather I'd left behind.

Dad had asked his old Greek business associate to meet me and take me to the hotel. The next day I'd catch a bus to my new home in a village in the mountains, where I would meet my new employer—a Greek woman who'd been running an English language school for more than twenty years.

"*Yeiasou!*" yelled an elderly, balding and rather large Greek man as I exited the customs hall. Clearly he recognised me…and I had a sudden memory of him— Stamatis: I was seven years old on holiday on a Greek island and he was making me cry as he told me off for climbing onto the unprotected side of his yacht.

Yes, that's him…the old coot, I remembered him shaking and scolding me, telling me that I could've been badly injured falling down the side and becoming trapped between two boats.

"He's only worried about you," Mum had soothed, shooting Dad a look that prompted him to go and have a word with his friend. "He didn't mean to make you cry…he's just being Greek." At seven years old, I didn't understand what she meant…but had sniffled a shy smile as he'd wandered over to pat my head and boom "You're a big girl, don't be so sad…come now, let's look at the fish."

Now I accepted his offer to take my luggage, and became aware of his eyes roving up and down my frame. *My God, I'm the daughter of his best English friend, and here he is, sizing me up!* Something else to add to the list of things not to tell my father. "Your father is an excellent man," Stamatis claimed as we drove out of the airport. "But why he wanted to stay in that dump of a hotel in Piraeus when he came here on business, and not in Central Athens at the Intercontinental, is beyond me."

Well, clearly he's a humbler and better man than you'll ever be…I bit my tongue and smiling sweetly, politely responded "You know Dad. Never one to want to show off." After all, despite yelling at me when I was younger and giving me the once over, he had met me from the airport and was driving me to "that dump in Piraeus" so I could stay in the same hotel Dad patronized twenty years ago. It wouldn't be fair of me to be rude to Stamatis, regardless of his lack of tact. Also, not really fair to hold onto a grudge about shouting at a seven year old version of me! So I shut up, took in my surroundings and allowed myself to be dropped off at my resting point.

"It is good to see you again, Rachel." Stamatis

hugged me, jumped into his 4-wheel-drive and sped off. *Thank God he didn't grab my arse. How would I have explained decking an old man?*

Contrary to Stamatis' disparaging comments, the hotel was no dump at all. Built on a hill outside Piraeus, it towered above the port and I allowed a shiver of excitement to run through me: *My first night in Greece!*

The next morning, squinting one eye shut against the daylight shining in through a crack in the curtains of my seventh-floor room, I could make out the sea and distant islands. Everything was bathed in bright sunlight—something of a novelty for me given that less than 24 hours ago, it had been a typically wet and grey English day. Still lying on my double bed, I rolled over and gazed at the view from the window. After a moment of allowing myself to bask in the sunlight from my vantage point, I stretched and padded out onto the balcony, marvelling at how clear and blue everything was. The hotel's location meant I could witness the hustle and bustle of the ferries below, unloading and loading—one pulling out to head to a visible island in the distance.

A glance at the bedside clock told me it was still only seven a.m., yet the street below was clogged with traffic, with horns blaring and people shouting at each other. I could distinctly hear raised voices and banging of fists on car bonnets. Leaning over my balcony, I saw two men shouting, waving and gesticulating at each other. They looked ready to break into a fight any minute. Yet suddenly, they broke out into raucous laughter and clapped one another on the back. *If this is how they carry on when they're happy, they must be ready to kill each other when they're angry.*

Making my way to the dining room on the ground floor, I gazed out through the floor to ceiling window whilst eating a Greek buffet breakfast of yogurt with honey and muesli, listening to the cacophony of shouts, laughter and car horns around me.

Later, as I was checking out, the receptionist behind the small wooden desk smiled: "Just stand outside, Madam. A yellow taxi will soon stop for you. Tell them you need to go to the bus station…and welcome to Greece" she added as an afterthought.

I smiled: *Yes, welcome to Greece, Rachel.*

Standing in the doorway of my new flat, I mulled over the last six hours. A taxi 'stopping for me' wasn't as easy as just standing outside the hotel, as the receptionist seemed to think. I'd had to endure half a dozen variations of "*Kyria,* that particular bus station is miles from here, *oxi.*" ("Madam, that place is on the other side of the planet, I'm not going there"), but I finally managed to persuade one to take me. Clearly there was more than one bus station in Athens, and mine was so far from Piraeus, no-one'd wanted to bother. *No priority in this country for a lone woman traveller then!* I'd identified the correct bus for my destination after struggling to decipher the Greek letters on the front. A snort from the bus driver with a vague nod of the head also confirmed it. Clearly in Greece, the passengers weren't accorded a great deal of courtesy from taxi drivers, nor public transport employees. A three hour journey took me to the inland village that'd be my new home for the next year. As my new boss had been lax in corresponding, I had no idea whether or not I'd be met, and no idea what to do when I arrived.

I'm thirty-four years old. I can do this. I do not need someone to hold my hand every step of the way I repeated this until it became a litany in my head. In any case, what could happen to me in a small town in the heart of Greece? I'd always wanted this; craved an adventurous life over stability. I was determined not to fall at the first hurdle. Unfortunately my imagination, whilst at times a blessing, could also occasionally serve as a curse. Images from the old Burt Reynolds movie *Deliverance* came to mind: inbred locals with matted hair cackling at me from the roadside as the bus trundled along, with the Appalachian Mountains of America replaced by bright limestone and strong sunlight of mainland Greece. But the drive—a slow meander into the mountains of Central Greece, the built up balconied apartment blocks of the city soon giving way to single story farms and pine forests—didn't produce any weird-looking locals along the way and I arrived at the village in the middle of a warm afternoon. I climbed down from the bus and found myself distracted from worrying about what to do next by the view...I stared at the mountain just ahead. The sun picked out the snow on its peak. *Even in September in Greece, there's snow.*

"*Kyria* Rachel?" enquired a very short lady in her forties with black bobbed hair and glasses that almost took up her entire face. "Me Anthoula, me sister of your boss man," she said as she struggled to take my huge case from under the bus. With a year's supply of clothes, my case was twice as big as her, and she seemed intent on picking it up and carrying it to God knows where.

I turned and smiled down at her, after figuring out she was the sister-in-law of my boss, and pointed to the wheels at the bottom, extending the trolley handle. Anthoula raised her eyes to the heavens and stretched out her palm vertically next to the side of her head. She then shook it rapidly from side to side, as if to indicate that she was a silly lady for not having figured this out herself.

It took ten minutes to manoeuvre the oversized suitcase into a waiting Volkswagen Polo. All the while, I watched people greeting each other with hugs, kisses and cheek pinching—my trance only broken when I heard Anthoula beckoning me from the car.

"Parnassos," Anthoula saw me looking at the mountain. "*Oreia*, eh?" Having picked up that "*oreia*" meant "beautiful" from my earlier years in Greece, I nodded. Mount Parnassos was, indeed, *oreia*. I could make out pine trees clustered up to a certain point, and then this gave way to the snow I'd seen earlier.

Anthoula dropped me at my flat and I stood in its doorway, taking in the main room with the single bed, desk, mirror, bookshelf and TV, as well as the separate kitchen and bathroom. The excitement of the last twenty-four hours was wearing off and I could feel my adrenaline and energy levels dropping. In their place I felt tears welling. It seemed as if the walls were closing in on me from all sides. If they'd been padded, it would have completed the illusion of an asylum. Anthoula had been sweet, but I still felt she'd simply dumped me here and expected me to fend for myself.

"Later," she'd said, patting me on the arm and unlocking the door to my new home. She'd placed the keys into my hands and scuttled off. My fridge was as bare as the walls; no milk, not even water. *Maybe Kirsty was right—I'm a failure at anything new I try.* Kirsty's words crept into my head—as they always do when I feel uncertain of my choices.

I looked out of the one window. Backing onto a small yard with an orange tree, at least I had something of a view: I told myself not to give in to negativity. *Kirsty can't hurt or affect you anymore. You're a big girl; deep breaths...get some sleep.* I was overwhelmed with exhaustion, and I knew that was making things look worse than they were. I liked my saner counterpart when it spoke out...it was a voice that made sense. I poked around some more and found, to my relief in the wardrobe in the corridor, a whole host of clean, fresh bed linen. I made up the bed and fell on top of it. Within minutes I was fast asleep, dreaming of ten year olds with matted hair knocking on my window.

The knocking turned out to be no dream. As I came to, cob-webbed from a deep afternoon nap, I realised that someone was, in fact, knocking at the window. It was a different lady this time: medium height, about fifty with shoulder-length blonde hair dappled with grey, wearing a flowery apron around her ample frame. This lady came laden with goods.

" *Yeiasou* Rachel, *me lene* Vasiliki." Vasiliki turned out to be my new boss's sister, and had bought a plate of spaghetti, a jar of honey, some Melba toasts...and milk!

Finally I could make that much needed cup of tea.

I unburdened Vasiliki of her load and planted kisses on both her cheeks. I'd read that this was the Greek way of greeting and thanking others. Vasiliki, in turn, held me at arm's length and proceeded to spit at me, three times: *ftou, ftou, ftou.* Here in the village, at seven p.m. on my first evening, a kind woman who'd brought food and milk for my tea had just spat at me! I became aware that it must be some kind of Greek custom as Vasiliki kept repeating *"Oreia, oreia"* and grinning at me whilst rubbing my arm.

I assumed it wasn't supposed to be insulting, but the arm rub on its own would've sufficed. I wasn't too sure how much spittle had landed on my plate of food, but I smiled back, trying to keep the shock from my face and act as if older Greek women spat at me all the time.

Having slept for most of the afternoon, I was now feeling more positive, especially as Vasiliki had just brought me food. Further inspection of the flat revealed a cupboard in the kitchen full of coffee and other useful day-to-day items such as crackers, bottled water, sugar and olive oil. While the water boiled I sat at the kitchen table and munched on the spaghetti, trying to ignore the fact that Vasiliki's welcoming phlegm might be lurking somewhere within the sauce, whilst congratulating myself on having packed the teabags.

I was glad I swallowed my pride and paid the excess baggage charge. For these small home comforts, it'd been worth it.

At ten p.m. another rap came on the window. This time a lady's voice called out in English, "Miss Rachel? Are you still awake? It's Mrs Stella, your new boss." I realised quickly that 'Stella' wasn't her surname…because she was formally introducing herself, I was to refer to her by her first name and her title.

I had cleared my plate, washed up and was trying to decipher the dials on the washing machine, so yes, I was definitely still awake. I ran my fingers through my hair in an attempt to look presentable and opened the door to let Mrs Stella in…only to try to stifle the urge to laugh out loud. Next to Mrs Stella—who loomed at least six feet tall with a severe bobbed haircut (what was it about bobs in this country?)—stood her husband Mr Ioannis, measuring in at about five feet two. With his hair mussed up, he looked a bit like a bewildered Einstein. His glasses seemed to be held together with duct tape.

Oh God, I've walked into a freak show. I felt a bit guilty thinking such disrespectful thoughts, but I couldn't help it—the size difference was just too striking.

"Come up to the house and have coffee with us," invited Mrs Stella. Mr Ioannis spoke no English, but no language was needed to understand him at that moment as he gave me the same once-over that Stamatis had subjected me to. I gave a mental shrug and decided then and there that trying to be all liberal would be wasted in this country. My immediate opinion of Mrs Stella was that she was a woman you didn't say no to, so the "offer" to come up for coffee was more an order than an invitation. I really didn't feel like making small talk to my new boss on my very first evening, dressed as I was in jogging pants and hoodie. Nevertheless, I followed them upstairs to their flat, more curious than anything else.

Mrs Stella's home was much more sumptuous in comparison to my little place. Settling onto a couch with big purple cushions, trying not to spill coffee as I sank back and wondered if it'd be considered rude to dunk the biscuits they proffered, I tried not to show my tiredness by yawning as Mrs Stella explained in her curt manner:

"You need not teach tomorrow, but come into school nevertheless. You can meet the children and the other teachers and introduce yourself. I trust Anthoula met you at the bus station? I would have come myself, but the days are busy with school preparation."

Although a serious person, Mrs Stella at least seemed fair. Her husband sat next to her and occasionally nodded his head as she spoke, casting surreptitious glances at me, glances I felt weren't in any way lecherous, so I saw no need to bleach myself in the shower afterwards or check the lock on my front door.

Do Greek men size women up all the time? Perhaps they're not even aware they do it. Maybe that's why my boss seemed such a harsh woman, if she's had to put up with being married to this kind of man all her life.

"Our school is called a *Frontesterion*. There are many of these in Greece. The children come here in the afternoons after their normal school hours. We operate from four until ten p.m." I gasped inwardly. The children must be exhausted by the end of the day. "So your timetable will start in the late afternoon."

"Why the need for extra schooling?" I enquired, realising this might be an insulting question, considering Mrs Stella owned and ran her own *Frontesterion*. I attempted to backtrack.

"It is alright, it is a good question. For many years now, English is a very necessary subject to study, but students only receive one hour of tuition in this subject a week in the state system, so schools like ours are a necessity."

If the state system was improved, maybe there'd be no need for all this extra study. The poor kids. I kept this to myself: without the *Frontesterion* system, I'd have no job in my 'dream' country after all.

"You like feta?" Mr Ioannis suddenly piped up. He went off to the kitchen, returning with a big plate of it. I thanked him, somewhat taken aback at the fact that Mr Ioannis seemed a bit of a dark horse and could understand more English than he made out, and that his first words to me had been about feta cheese. Nevertheless, it'd taste great tomorrow morning on the crackers, drizzled with honey.

"My husband is the Assistant Town Mayor here," Mrs Stella explained as our evening coffee was interrupted by phone calls from people asking for favours and Mr Ioannis wheeling and dealing his way through the calls.

Returning to my little flat at around midnight—after being led to the door by the elbow and a polite "*Kali nichta,*"—no cheek kissing from my boss then—I felt grateful that she was breaking me in gently. *Or maybe she's fattening me up, giving me false confidence before the kill? I guess I'll find out tomorrow.* Those were the last thoughts I had before drifting off to sleep.

Chαptεr 3

The next morning I noticed an immediate difference between waking up at the Piraeus hotel and in my new basement flat: blue skies and twinkling sea vs. lack of sunlight in a one-windowed, marble-floored room. And what was this? I craned my neck out of the window and stared at the slope on which the house perched.

"Bloody hell!" I hadn't realised just how steep the road outside was, and was grateful that Anthoula had met me at the bus station the previous day.

I'd planned for a mini-adventure tour of the surroundings before school, but sleeping late meant I now only had time to shower (after I'd figured out how to turn the hot water tank on), eat crackers with cheese and honey, and choose suitable clothes. I rummaged around in my as yet unpacked suitcase. "Not sure about the jeans, and it looks too warm for a button down shirt..." I muttered as I threw aside each item, making a big pile on the floor.

Eventually, dressed in my trademark black trousers, dark polo neck and purple scarf, I waited by Mrs Stella's car—how it didn't roll down the hillside, physics can't explain—chewing on a thumbnail. I knew I was well trained and prepared for this, and had managed to dress the part—conservatively I thought best—but even so, entering a classroom for the first time would still be nerve-racking. Eventually Mrs Stella emerged from her front door and strolled to the car.

"Have you been waiting long?" she asked, leaning in to the wing mirror to check her hair.

"Oh, you know, I got here on time," I smiled, figuring this was the most diplomatic way of saying that yes, I'd been waiting for a while yet not wanting to alienate my boss on the first day. I figured there were two kinds of time in Greece: the "stated" and the "actual." For example, if a Greek proposed to meet you at ten a.m., you should start getting ready at ten, and even then you'd probably be early when you eventually turned up at the rendezvous point at half past.

"Good, let's go then."

As I climbed into the passenger seat I looked up at the house and saw Vasiliki waving at me from the window. I smiled and waved back: at least my boss's sister was friendly.

The journey was a fifteen minute ride to the next village, even smaller than the one where I lived. I managed to still my nerves by marvelling at the scenery: We were driving at an angle to Parnassos, past cotton fields with windfarms above them on the hilltops. There were small tavernas dotting the roadside, and cafes where men sat outside fiddling with worry beads. I took it all in, noting how different the commute was compared to life in the UK, and realised that if I were to settle comfortably into Greek life, I'd have to loosen up a lot and lose my grip on my English-isms—timekeeping would be a good start.

We pulled up outside a one storey structure...a

winding metal staircase leading up to a flat roof which held the obligatory solar panels, so often seen on Greek buildings. The name of the school was painted in black letters across the front, and I felt a brief flicker of disappointment. I had a romanticized notion that all buildings in Greece were white with blue shutters. This one had been white once, but paint crumbled from the walls and there was no sign of any shutters, let alone blue ones. I did notice the ivy creeping up around the spiral roof staircase though, and the opposite side of the building looked as if a bougainvillea plant was trying to blossom into life. The building was small: two classrooms in the windowless basement, a room with a photocopier in it and three classrooms on the ground floor), and after a brief tour I found myself shuttled into the tiny staffroom to meet the other four teachers—all Greeks who were chattering away to each other, nursing delicious smelling small cups of coffee.

"Rachel will be with us this academic year," Mrs Stella announced by way of introduction. They all stopped talking and turned to me with looks that seemed to say *"and?"* just as I heard the staff room door click closed as Mrs Stella left. She had left pretty swiftly.

I suppose I couldn't expect them to jump for joy just because I was the new English teacher. I remembered my promise to adapt. *Don't let your subconscious colonial heritage make you feel superior,* I thought. After all, the school hired a new native English teacher every year, so my face was just one of the many they'd seen come and go. And the teachers weren't exactly rude, they were just…indifferent. The three women and one man regarded me with a *"been there done that—let's see how this one fares"* expression…a wry smile revealing their inner thoughts. Eventually one piped up.

"Manos." He extended his hand to shake mine.

"Helena." Helena did the same.

"Eleni." Eleni stayed seated, but at least she offered a friendly smile.

"Alexandra." The same reaction as Eleni's, minus the smile.

"Hi," I replied, offering my own smile. I figured I could at least appear friendly and accommodating, not like the stiff-upper-lip Brit they might be used to. A paranoid part of me thought *Oh God, they can see I'm new to teaching and look as if they're going to relish seeing me eaten alive by the students!*

"So that's the introductions over and done with," Mrs Stella re-entered the staff room, almost as if she'd been listening at the door. The other teachers kept quiet and returned to marking essays or preparing lesson plans, avoiding eye contact. "Ready to meet the students?"

"Don't worry," she said as she steered me towards the classroom. "I have great faith in you. You've already travelled to many places and taught abroad before; this shows me you can adjust to any new situation. It's a trait that has to naturally be a part of a person's character—it cannot be taught. You'll adapt to this situation just fine, and the students will learn a lot from you."

I cringed inwardly, remembering my only previous teaching experience as a volunteer in Sri Lanka—where I'd spent most of the time showing the kids pictures of red telephone boxes, London buses and black cabs.

"And don't worry about the teachers—they are shy of their English language abilities in front of a native teacher," she concluded. This was probably the longest speech Mrs Stella had made so far. All pumped up with adrenaline, I strode into the classroom with a sense of pride…only to have my balloon popped when I was greeted by a group of thirteen bored, indifferent-looking teenagers.

Mrs Stella had to nudge me through the door, since the shock of seeing so many blank faces had frozen me to the spot. I composed myself and turned to thank my boss for those last inspiring words, only for the second time that day to hear the door click shut behind me. And was that the sound of the key turning? No, just my imagination, as I discovered when I tried the handle.

Drawing a deep breath, I turned and strode to the front of the class, exuding more confidence than I actually felt. All eyes followed me as I placed my carefully prepared "Introduction to Me" materials on the small desk.

And, what was this—a *blackboard*? My training had used fancy interactive whiteboards with internet access. The nearest thing to technology in this classroom was going to be the light switch. And something else was odd—what was that noise? Turning toward the offending sound, I discovered that thirteen jaws were chomping to the rhythm of some unheard tune. The whole class was chewing gum, and doing so rather loudly. Okay, something had to be done, and fast.

I took the bull by the horns. "Start tough; later you can back down," had been the advice of my tutor, Gloria, and now I fully intended to follow it.

"Hi. My name's Rachel. You've probably guessed I'm from England. But I am slightly confused—I thought

I was to be your English teacher," I started.

A slight murmur stirred the classroom. One boy shouted from the back, "You are, why you say that?" In actual fact, as I'd discovered in my short time in Greece, he was speaking at a normal Grecian pitch, but to my ears and my heightened sensitivity and nerves on that first day, it felt more like a shout.

"Because I wonder if I am, in fact, a farmer—here to take the cows in to be milked," I attempted a joke, wondering if they would understand such a dry observation, or if it might be a little too sarcastic for them.

Confusion flickered across their faces as another student, this time a girl with an unfortunate case of acne, dared to venture the question I'd been expecting: "You are saying we are like cows, *Kyria* Rachel?"

"Well, yes," I replied. "Looking at you, all I see are cows chewing on grass. Listen to you, chomping your gum; you look and you sound like cows chewing the cud! Remove it, please."

My aim was not to break the number one rule of teaching by throwing sarcasm at them; it was to introduce the students to an idiomatic phrase—they were learning English on the hoof, as it were. The cattle metaphors were blossoming nicely. Picking up the rubbish bin, I meandered among the tables, congratulating myself that the students were actually tossing their wads of gum into it—albeit with mumbles of Greek under their breath.

"Thank you," I beamed as the last piece plunked into the bin. "In future, I'd appreciate it if you removed your gum before entering my classroom." A few students nodded in assent, but most looked curiously at this new teacher who'd referred to them as cows and considered herself a farmer.

Meanwhile, I was marvelling at how well I'd handled myself, and how well the average sixteen-year-old Greek student understood English. Maybe the actual teaching part wouldn't be too hard after all. Perhaps the challenge will be winning my students' hearts and minds. I might be new to teaching, but I wasn't a fool. I was aware that it would be important to treat my protégées with respect as human beings, to *listen* to them, yet maintain professional distance and not become their friend. Turning back to the class, I relished this latter challenge and looked forward to getting to know their personalities and nurture their abilities.

"Good," I continued. "Now that's over, let's get on with introducing ourselves. I'm not going to actually be teaching you today, but I am sure you're dying to know all about me."

"Not really," mumbled an attractive boy at the back—the one who'd responded to my earlier comment about being here to teach and not to farm. Even though he was seated, it was obvious he was tall. And with his olive-coloured skin, his short-cropped jet black hair and his remarkable blue eyes (blue? I thought Greeks had brown eyes. In that instant I was struck by his exotic-ness), I realised I'd have my work cut out with this one. I made a mental note to rearrange the seating of these students before class met again and not have him sat at the back.

"And you are ...?" I gave him an open smile, intended to be neither hostile nor challenging.

"He's *malaka*," replied the acne-covered girl. Oblivious to what this word meant, I assumed this was the Adonis' name.

"Pleased to meet you, *Malaka*." The hoots and whistles that followed this exchange soon alerted me that this was probably *not* the thing to have said.

"*Kyria* Rachel, do you understand that *malaka* is not a word you should to be going around saying?" queried a third student, confirming my realisations.

There were two ways I could handle this. I could become outraged that they'd upstaged me, or I could go along with it. I thought quickly, but it turned out I needn't to do either as the Adonis (who was, in fact, named Konstantinos) retorted to the rest of the class, "Be quiet and listen to the new *Kyria*."

Clearly he felt bad that he'd caused embarrassment to his new teacher, so he was now working to bring the situation back under control. Their amusement at my expense subsided and I began to discover more about Konstantinos, Litza, (the girl who'd translated *malaka*), Dimitra (the girl with acne) and the rest of the class. All in all, my introductory lesson was a success. The hour flew by, and I heard an old-fashioned hand rung bell that signalled the end of the lesson, far sooner than expected. *So the blackboard isn't the only non-technological item here.* It felt rather quaint; to be teaching in a remote village with ivy, bougainvillea, blackboards and hand-held bells.

Smiling as I said goodbye to them all, Konstantinos and Dimitra told me they'd see me tomorrow. "Try to remember my correct name, *Kyria*," was Konstantinos' cheeky parting comment as he left the classroom.

One introduction class down, only one more to go before I had to leave for the day. Just enough time to munch on a digestive biscuit before the next lot arrives. (As I'd thought, digestives had been another luxury I'd packed from home. I'd lied before; I'd have paid £90 in excess baggage fees.)

A knock on the door announced Mrs Stella's arrival. "So, how did your introduction with the teenagers go…any problems that I should know about?" I was about to open my mouth and mention Konstantinos when I noticed him hovering behind Mrs Stella in the open classroom doorway. He was trying to communicate something with his eyes whilst shaking his head. Stopping in my tracks, I returned my attention to Mrs Stella and smiled.

"They took a while to warm to me, but I think in time we'll be okay," I replied. The relief in Konstantinos's eyes was obvious as Mrs Stella agreed. She added, "Do not take *any* nonsense from Konstantinos—the good-looking boy with the blue eyes. If you have any problems with him, send him to me immediately."

I glanced over to see him slink away from the door. I realised that these kids, even the formidable Konstantinos, were afraid of my boss. I wondered if the other teachers were also overawed by her, contributing to their silence and that lack of eye-contact when I met them.

"Ready for the next lot?" asked Mrs Stella. She jerked her head in the vague direction of a dozen nine-year-olds who were lining up outside the classroom. They trooped in, giggling and whispering to each other as they eyed me.

"I'll do a little introduction, as their English knowledge is a little less advanced than the other class."

While my boss (who managed to look stern, even

when not telling someone off) was introducing me, I looked at the little faces in the room: they seemed much more open and inquisitive than those of the teenage class.

The rest of the day ran quite smoothly, and later on I sat in a pool of fading sunlight in the tiny courtyard at the back of my flat. The courtyard had an orange and lemon tree growing in it, and picking an orange from the tree, I peeled it and sunk my teeth into what I anticipated would be a sweet orange. My gag reflexes went into hyperdrive as I spat the bitter fruit out. What I had absent-mindedly ingested was not an orange, but a *neranzi*—bitter orange used to make jams and desserts, but never eaten raw. *Oh well, isn't this what living in a foreign culture's all about—experiencing weird and wonderful things?* I thought, although my mouth wasn't quite agreeing with this internal dialogue.

The "little ones," as I thought of them, had a surprisingly good command of English for their age. Most had been attending pre-school since the age of four. My lesson with this age group also helped me to understand the silence of at least one of the other teachers: Helena only taught this age group and I concluded that after a few hours of teaching the younger children, she was more exhausted than indifferent.

The children had been attentive, listening to me tell them where I was from and what I'd done before becoming a teacher. When it was their turn to ask me things, they fired questions at me in "Gringlish," a marked contrast to the teens. And at least they weren't chewing gum. The funniest question was from a young girl named Bettina:

"*Kyria* Rachel, has your family died?" she enquired in her pidgin English.

"Excuse me?" After some coaxing from the others it became clear that Bettina, like most of the others, was wondering if one of my family members had passed away because I was wearing so much black. This explained all their tiny whisperings when I'd entered the classroom. It was then I learned about the Greek tradition of wearing black during times of mourning.

When a member of a woman's family dies, she wears black for a period of time. In traditional Greek families, when a woman's husband dies, the widow wears black for the rest of her life. This practice contrasted strongly with that of the men, who wear only a black armband for a short period after the death of a wife. It also explained the typical picture postcard scenes of old Greek women dressed in black.

I didn't have the heart to tell the children that no, the only reason I was wearing black was because I felt it made me look slimmer…it suddenly seemed so shallow and materialistic. So I uttered the first thought that came to mind:

"Yes, my older sister," I said, crossing my fingers behind my back.

"Never mind," Bettina piped up, "you are still beautiful, Miss." I smiled at her implication. At least I was more attractive in this girl's eyes than a dead person.

Chapter 4

Glancing at the bedside clock, I groaned. It was only half past eight, and there was no need to leave for school until two. I forced myself out of bed anyway, determined to have a nose around my new neighbourhood.

After a long shower in my tiled bathroom that resembled something out of the 1970s (a disco ball wouldn't have fitted into my luggage along with the teabags, otherwise the party would've been complete), I pulled on casual clothes and set off down the hill. It wasn't lost on me how blue the skies were, and the mountain in the distance teased me with its snow-peaked presence.

My first human encounter in the village was with an old man, sitting outside his shop halfway down the hill—my street—that sold heating oil. An open fronted affair, the shop resembled a car mechanic's workshop, but with bottled oil instead. The man was sitting on a wicker chair outside the shuttered entrance. Spotting me, he rose, waved me over and proceeded to rub my cheeks and try to embrace me, all the while chattering away in Greek.

"I can't understand a word you're saying," I kept repeating as I backed away from his open arms, but it was no good: he carried on talking in rapid Greek. I soon managed to decipher a few words—*"Kyria Stella"* and *"Scholeio Anglia."*

He must know I'm staying in my boss's house and that I'm the new English teacher. I smiled a lot and promised that yes, one day I would join him for a glass of tea and honey...that's what he'd been drinking and had kept trying to push into my hands. After about five minutes of this confusing but not unpleasant toing and froing, I continued on down the hill, eager to see all that the village had to offer. At least he hadn't spat at me.

My next encounter was not so smooth; a Greek woman in her mid-20s was crossing the street at the bottom of the hill, looking in the opposite direction. My first meeting with Kaliopi was to almost bowl her over as the momentum of my descent wouldn't let me stop, but it was a meeting that was to launch a lasting friendship.

"Sorry, sorry, sorry!" I stammered whilst checking to see if the woman was all right. I wasn't sure if she understood me, although it was clear I was genuinely sorry by the fact I was trying to brush her down. Tall, thin with large brown eyes and short black hair, she looked me up and down. After an awkward pause she burst out laughing and hugged me hard...*these Greeks appear to enjoy embracing.*

"Hi, I'm Kaliopi," she said in perfect English. Taking my hand, this exuberant Greek pulled me along, "Come with me, you look like you need a cup of strong Greek coffee."

"How do you know I'm English?" I asked.

"Please. Have you looked in the mirror? Have you compared yourself with people around here? You at least look like you have...*some* style..." she paused. "I am not stupid, you know." She tossed her head and gave a snort, turning her attention back to the task in hand: taking me for coffee.

I got the impression she didn't rate the local population very highly, and I guessed that like Mrs Stella, Kaliopi wasn't a lady you said "no" to. Deciding to fall in line with this new turn of events, I followed her down the narrow, cobbled street.

Passing the butcher's—huge carcasses of pigs hanging in the window with their heads still on—and baker's shop—delicious smells of bread wafting out to greet us, along with the whistling baker, I almost expected to find a candlestick maker's as well. It felt very quaint.

We passed several small haberdasheries with old women dressed in black crouched low behind the counter, but no supermarkets that sold everything under one roof. It was part of this small town's appeal—the giants of capitalism hadn't appeared to impose their presence and wipe out local trade. And there were no Golden Arches to spoil the view either. Instead there were small cafés selling their own chicken and pork dishes as well as home-made burgers. And apart from the narrow high street for cars, the side streets were all cobbled. It literally felt as if I'd stepped into a Dickens novel.

"Don't worry," Kaliopi glanced at my face, "There's a Lidl at the edge of town. I go there sometimes to shop, so we can go together from now on." *Ah, so not entirely free of the supermarket giants, then.* Apparently it was easy to make a new friend here, not forgetting the old man and his oil shop. I almost expected to find the Greek equivalent of five "Bridesmaids" by the time the day was through.

At the end of the village the small main road led off to the right, heading out of town, but Kaliopi led me to the left, away from the shops and through a different part of town—an area that resembled a small nature reserve that boasted a gushing river, several cafés and a cobbled pedestrian walkway that meandered first into a wooded area and then up to a ruined castle. We found a small café with tables outside and in. "Here—sit here in the sunshine. I know that you English people love to get your skin all brown and wrinkly for some reason." She ordered from the waiter as she moved her chair into the shade of a large tree: tea and a large piece of baklava.

"I have also requested you some milk, as I know you English love to milk in everything," she said in her mixture of formal and Pidgin English. "And on third thoughts, you don't look ready for our coffee," she sniffed, giving me the once over.

"And for you?" I asked, relaxing into my surroundings and choosing to ignore her strange comment about Greek coffee. Maybe it was this odd girl's sense of humour. I didn't want to presume to correct her English. I wasn't there to teach her, and besides, she was a bit scary!

"Me? Oh nothing, I took my breakfast this morning, after I returned from my six a.m. three-kilo run." *Kilometre, it's kilometre*—but I didn't correct her. I must have responded with a look of horror, because Kaliopi added, "I walked most of the way. And now I have the opportunity to show off to a foreigner what little there is to do in this hole from hell, and also to practise in my English. This is perfect for me! Don't worry, I won't ask you to be joining me on the runs. I know how unfit you British are—you always eating the fatty things for breakfast. Frying with the vegetable oil bread and eggs and those sausage things…what is wrong with you?"

I didn't really have the chance to answer as it appeared from our interactions so far that most of Kaliopi's questions were rhetorical, so I smiled inwardly and allowed myself the luxury of soaking up the atmosphere, content to let her chatter away. *Within the space of forty -eight hours I'm sitting outside a café by the river on a gloriously warm September morning with a very interesting "local",* I thought, gazing out to the river. I caught sight of a marble woman's head poking up from the depths and pointed this out to my new friend.

"She's *Herkyna*. This area we're in now is called *Krya*. Legend has it that *Herkyna* used to play here with her friend *Persephone*. *Herkyna* was holding a goose and suddenly it flew away into a cave. *Persephone* rushed after it, but the water suddenly rose, trapping *Persephone* inside it and carrying her to the Underworld. The marble head honours this legend."

The area we were seated in was beautifully lush and green—there was no mistaking the rushing sound of water—and to my right, just in front of the wooded area, an old mill with a waterwheel completed the scene of tranquillity.

I tuned back to Kaliopi's conversation. "I come from a small town by the coast in the Peloponnese. My father still lives there, but we have a place in Athens also," she developed a faraway look in her eyes. "My mother died when I was young, leaving him and my two other sisters—I am the middle."

The subject must've been a sensitive one as Kaliopi changed it abruptly. Her distant look cleared and as she shook her head as if to clear it, snapping back to the present and said, "Why don't you come to my Athens home this weekend, so we can escape this place?" *Seriously, I've just met this girl and she's inviting me to her home? And she's got two of them?*

"You must be incredibly rich."

"Pah! In Greece, many people keep their family homes in their village for generations and pass them on down the family line. They also have a place in the city where they move to work. Rarely do people take out these mortgage things. I am amazed to learn that in your country, people continue into their fifties to owe banks for their homes...the banks own you, can you not see that?"

I guess I'd never really looked at it like that...I'd always seen taking out a bank loan to buy a house as the norm. Kaliopi's father lived in the Peloponnese family home whilst she stayed in the Athens apartment, and it appeared they owned these outright.

"I used to work in the city, but I changed jobs. I'm only in this hole from hell village renting a place because the bank I work for has no vacancies in my line of work in Athens at the moment, but they did here." She wrinkled her nose in disgust. "I need to prove to those *malakas* in Head Office that I am—how you say? Bendy, that's it—I must work in this place until a vacancy arises back in civilization." This exchange had been emphasized with a variety of gestures that ended with her ramming her index finger with finality onto the table and sweeping her arm around her. *She really doesn't like it here...and*

what does she mean by being 'bendy?' I already understood *malakas*, thanks to my introduction with the teens
yesterday.

"Ah, Kaliopi, I think you mean you're being *flexible*," I stifled a laugh as I decided that now might be a
good opportunity to correct her English.

"Yes, bendy, flexible—what is the difference?"
Kaliopi shrugged, regarding me with one eye closed
against her cigarette smoke.

"Well, bendy refers to a person's suppleness and..."
I smiled, deciding to let the matter drop. I didn't intend
to put my teacher's hat on right this minute, and besides
Kaliopi looked in danger of dropping off to sleep.

We ate in silence for a while. "I need your advice,"
Kaliopi suddenly perked up. "After all, you are a
foreigner and not from the village, so you are sane and
will have a more open mind and not judge me, since
you've just met me. I had a man spend last Friday night
at my flat in Athens. Then on Saturday, my other male
friend came to stay. Was it impolite for me not to change
the bed sheets after the first man?"

Spluttering on my drink, I wondered if the question was once again a rhetorical one, or if it actually
required an answer. The dilemma seemed to resolve
itself as Kaliopi continued, "I think in future I must
change the sheets when this happens. I cannot have them
smelling of different men; it is not the proper way for a
young lady to conduct herself." I glanced at her; she was
in a world of her own, quite content to be open and frank
with me, despite the fact we'd only known each other for
an hour. I was rapidly discovering Kaliopi's boundaries
were vastly different from mine, yet I found this refresh-

ing…*I wonder if this is a Greek thing or a Kaliopi thing?*

My second day at school went surprisingly well. Maybe my spirits had been lifted by my chance encounter with Kaliopi that morning. I hadn't seen Konstantinos or his entourage again, but a new group of kids in their early teens had been decidedly quieter than yesterday's classes, yet still keen to ask questions.

"You have seen the Big Ben, *Kyria*?" asked one boy.

"We don't use the definite article in front of 'Big…'" I started to explain, and then stopped and smiled…plenty of time for teaching verbs, and it was my first day with this particular class.

"Yes, I have. Big Ben is in which city?"

"The London in the England" a young girl proudly stated. *I'm going to have my work cut out for me*, I thought, but at least they weren't chewing gum and their geography's good.

"That's right," I said, and I gave them homework to write a small paragraph about what they knew about London and the UK.

I also seemed to develop a better rapport with the teachers today; "I live just around the corner from you," Manos said after a discussion in the staffroom. It turned out he was Greek Australian and had moved back to the motherland to be with his elderly parents. "I'll give you a lift back in the evening, save you waiting for a bus." He also introduced me to *spanakopita*—feta cheese and spinach pie.

"Just wait here, I won't be long." School had finished and we were on our way home. Manos gestured for me to stay sitting in his car as he stopped at a little roadside place at the edge of a cotton field, conversed with the owner for a few minutes and purchased something in a brown paper bag. *Is this some sort of inner Greek town mafia-style drug deal?* No, it's my imagination running riot again. It was merely a spinach pie. For some reason, I felt a little let down.

"Get that down you," Manos said in his slight Australian twang, tossing the paper bag onto my lap as he climbed back into the car. "It's the best around here."

He was right—I savoured the softness of the cheese, the slightly bitter tang of the spinach and what tasted like spring onions and yes, I certainly *did* get it down me: mostly the front of my shirt as the filo pastry crumbled everywhere.

Later, in bed, I rolled over and eyed the clock—midnight. I'd been home for two hours and made the mistake of making my first Greek coffee about an hour ago. Kaliopi's comments made me feel that I needed to prove her wrong, that I was ready for Greek coffee. Judging by the slight tremors in my hands, I didn't think it was a sign that I was going crazy (yet), nor that the *spanakopita* contained some sort of drug—rather that Greek coffee shouldn't be drunk so late at night.

Lying flat on my back with one arm bent over my eyes, I stared up at the ceiling and contemplated my day; delicious food and interesting characters. Bring it on.

Chapter 5

I'd finished work around seven that evening. "I'll take the bus tonight," Manos wasn't due to finish until nine.

"Have fun," he'd responded, grinning as he looked up from his marking. I gave him a questioning look, but he wouldn't elaborate further...I soon understood.

The small village where the school was located had the main highway to Athens cutting through the middle of it. I say 'highway'—this consisted of only two lanes. Outside a *periptero*—a small yellow kiosk found everywhere in Greece selling newspapers, magazines, cigarettes and sweets, the newsagent's equivalent—was a small shelter, a sign with a crudely drawn bus attached to it. This, I assumed correctly, was the bus stop.

Once on board, I saw most people were sitting on the aisle seat with their belongings stacked next to them, occupying the otherwise empty window seat. *Surely they'll just see me and move their things to make room*, I reasoned, but no, it seemed that Greek bus logic was different. I began to feel uncomfortable after standing beside a middle aged lady for half a minute, and the bus was on its way already. She showed no signs of moving or even acknowledging my existence, so I cleared my throat, pointed to the window seat beside her, and smiled. She slowly tilted her head in my direction, placed her sunglasses on top of her head and making direct eye contact, she snorted and indicated the row behind with a jab of her thumb. I glanced at the alternative suggestion, but the aisle seat next to the empty window seat was occupied by an Orthodox priest. *Is it taboo for a female to sit next to a priest?* I knew it wasn't allowed in Sri Lanka, so I once again pointed to the spare seat next to the woman. She responded by crossing her arms, closing her eyes, and pretending to fall asleep.

It was time to get down and dirty. I was fed up by this point, so grabbing the woman's belongings, I placed them in the overhead rack and squeezed myself into the seat next to her. I contemplated treading on her foot, but didn't, yet braced myself for some sort of retaliation, given my brazenness. I was surprised when she shuffled slightly to allow me to manoeuvre past—albeit with lots of tutting and muttering, but nothing worse. Clearly she didn't begrudge me doing any of her work and so, having won that particular round, I mentally licked my index finger and drew a 'one' in the air, smiling as the bus trundled through the growing dusk to the village. *Mastered the art of dealing with the locals on buses; don't take any rubbish from them.*

After a 15 minute ride, the bus pulled up outside a taverna in my village—this was our bus stop. Here I found Kaliopi standing in jogging pants and running shoes. I grinned at my new friend, who was bouncing up and down on the spot. She grabbed my hand, "Come. I've done another six kilo run and need a coffee and baklava…you're joining me."

"Kilometre Kaliopi, it's Kilometre" I decided her English education would start now.

"Yes, you and your bendy/flexible/kilo/kilo-metre...whatever. 'You say tom-*ah*-to, I say tom-*ay*-to' blah blah...let's just go get coffee."

"Go *and* get coffee..." I started, but stopped yet again with an internal shrug of my shoulders. Plenty of time to correct my bombastic friend.

Settling into our riverside spot with the refreshments, Kaliopi shook out a crumpled cigarette of some indeterminate local make, lit it with a disposable Bic and held it between her manicured fingers, attempting to blow a smoke ring, frowning as she failed to.

"A cigarette...after jogging?"

She patted my knee and blew smoke from the side of her mouth, "My dear, you haven't been in Greece long enough to know that everything about this country, including its people, is contradictory. Give it time; you'll see. Now, how was your second full day at school?"

I mentally rehashed my day:

"*Kyria* Rachel, thank you for saying not a thing to *Kyria* Stella, she likes to pull the ear" Konstantinos had said that afternoon. I hadn't had time to ponder if this was an exaggeration, a mis-use of the phrase 'pull my leg' (highly doubtful as I wouldn't have put Mrs Stella down as one to joke with her students—actually, not anyone come to that) or if it was possibly true—and I wouldn't put it past her. I didn't get time, however, to investigate if this was indeed the case because a few minutes later I'd had to separate Konstantinos and Dimitra—she'd been about to start throwing punches. Apparently Konstantinos had made an inappropriate comment about her mother.

My classroom looked out onto the back garden of

the school, still filled with summer flowers, a little over-grown but with a delightful lemon tree in the centre, I'd taken them by their wrists into the area and demanded, "OK, fight it out like proper adults then. Come on! What are you waiting for?" The other students all looked out of the window, eagerly awaiting the result. And was that a few Euro notes being swapped between a couple of people? Maybe they were placing bets. My ploy had worked though; I'd realised the situation could have gone either way—they would either simmer down, or fight, albeit verbally. Fortunately they chose the former. Looking at me as if I was slightly mad, (they'd still not recovered from the cow incident), Konstantinos and Dimitra had slunk back into the room, the rest back to their chairs (Euros exchanged back) and settled into an uneasy silence. I'd figured that the best thing was to beat my students at their own game. When working in a mental asylum, best to behave as if you're madder than the inmates, right?

Having (at least for the moment) defused the tension, and in the light of the near fracas that'd occurred, I'd proceeded to change the lesson plan. The class would discuss what attracts men and women to each other and then as a homework assignment, prepare a Personal Advertisement in English.

"I think two of my teenage students, who appear to detest each other, will end up getting married and having kids," I now told Kaliopi, "and I think that my boss doesn't like me." This was based on Mrs Stella's general demeanour.

"Ah," she said, dragging heavily on her cigarette and closing her eyes in bliss as she inhaled, "you are too sensitive. You have yet to toughen yourself to the Greek way of being. When we have something to say, we say it…unlike you British, who take an hour to come out with what they really want to say. Look at our language structure by comparison. Let's suppose you want to know the time."

"Ok then, ask me like I'm a stranger" I was intrigued.

"We'd simply ask you what the time is. You Brits use so much language! For example, 'Excuse me, but would you happen to have the time, please?' If you said that to a Greek, he'd probably reply, 'Yes, I do,' and then you would have to ask a follow up question, asking him to tell you what the time actually was. You people are so caught up with being polite and false and fake and nice to each other that you never get down to the point at hand. Your boss, it's that Mrs Stella woman right? Yes, she's known around these parts as being cold-hearted…I hear things at work…but she's also probably just being her normal self. I mean, she doesn't *dis*like you, how can she? She doesn't know you well enough yet to have formed an opinion. And if she doesn't like you, at least she's being honest to your face about it." Kaliopi said all of this without pausing for breath.

The barb about being too sensitive had stung— rather proving the point at hand. I grimaced slightly, but Kaliopi hadn't finished.

"Yes," she continued, "we here in Greece, we fight—how you say, like cat and mouse? —but at least we get it over and finished with. We scream. I tried to scratch my sister Stavroula's eyes out once," she reflected rather flippantly, her own eyes clouding at the memory.

"We throw things, but then it is finished. You people? You let things build inside of you for months on end. You hold—how you say, grudges—you know these grudge things that are unhealthy and ultimately lead to cancer?"

I desperately wanted to point out that the little white tube Kaliopi was dragging on as if her life depended on it was more likely to cause cancer, but I was starting to get a feel for my friend's character now—passionate about any topic she spoke about—and I didn't want to interrupt her flow. I also didn't have the energy at that moment to correct her English and tell her the expression was to 'fight like cat and dog.' Besides, I wondered if Kaliopi had a point: Do we hold onto things for too long? I had to admit that in my short time here, I'd certainly observed people blowing up at each other one minute, only to be friends the next—Konstantinos and Dimitra were a perfect example, as were the two men I'd observed that first morning from my hotel balcony in Piraeus.

We finished up our coffee (tea for me) and baklava, and then I meandered through the darkening streets of the village, back up the steep, steep hill to my little flat. Although it was growing dark, I didn't feel in any way threatened. People of all ages were still sitting outside cafés at tables on the pavement laughing, smoking, playing *tavli*. Kids as young as nine or ten years were running around. *This is nice. Young and old seem to mix all together. And I don't see many people ordering alcoholic drinks either.* Unlocking my front door I let out a gasp as I realised something; I'd been so caught up in the adventure of arriving and starting school, I'd neglected to call Dad and let him know how I was.

"Yes, Dad, my boss is fine. A bit cool, perhaps, but I'm beginning to get the hang of her." Restraining any comments about Stamatis, his pervert friend, I assured Dad that my arrival in Athens had gone without a hitch. "Yes, he collected me and took me to the hotel," was all I said.

"Your boss probably has very strong political views," replied Dad. "They all do in Greece."

I rolled my eyes and thanked God this was a voice and not video chat. Dad had always loved politics, and the phone conversation spared me a lecture about the history of Greece and how it shaped its present genera-tion, which would no doubt have taken place if this were a face-to-face discussion. Quite how Mrs Stella's cool-ness transmuted in my father's mind to a strong interest in politics was beyond me, but anyway…

My mind wandered back to the conversation. He was reminiscing about his experiences with the Greeks and their culture. Occasionally I had to bite my tongue: they weren't 'real' everyday Greeks…these were Greeks in the shipping world—the very rich who had a world-view quite different from that of the everyday citizen. I'd have loved Dad to meet the old man with his tea and honey down the street.

"Rachel love? What do you think?"

"I think I might like it here long term, Dad. I've met an interesting woman who I go for coffee with; she's helping to educate me in all things Greek."

"I thought you might," he observed. "Keep in touch sweetheart, and don't let the students get to you too much."

Autumn

Chapter 6

My time in the village began to settle into a routine. Every second Wednesday a *laiki*, or Farmer's Market came to town in the morning and took over the entire street at the bottom of the hill. If the village hadn't already made me feel as if I was far removed from British culture, the experience of this fortnightly event made me feel almost Mediterranean, even if I didn't need to buy anything, I looked forward to meandering through the stalls just to hear the cries of the fruit and vegetable sellers, marvel at the different products for sale—from fresh fruit and vegetables to lace lingerie. Elderly ladies dressed in black from head to toe came to haggle with the stall-holders whilst they in turn chased off young gypsy children trying to steal an apple or two.

Once the students at school became accustomed to my unorthodox methods, they soon settled and knuckled down to studying and learning.

The lesson following Konstantinos and Dimitra's fight proved interesting. They'd created their own personal advertisement (minus their names) and described themselves in a variety of ways: "Like disco" —I discovered this was Dimitra, "Like eating rabbit" —Konstantinos handed this to me with a wide grin. I pinned these up at the front of the classroom, divided into boy and girl sections and asked the girls to each choose a boy whose description sounded intriguing, and vice versa. Konstantinos and Dimitra picked each other, supporting my theory that they would, indeed, eventually marry and have many children.

"No Miss!" Dimitra wailed when she found out that the rabbit eater was her arch-enemy. She threw Konstantinos a look of disgust, which Konstantinos returned with interest.

I soon became aware, though, that they lacked any meaningful knowledge of the outside world.

"Paris is a great country city" I corrected a sentence in an essay from Litza. She could've just made an English language mistake, but it was best to set the record straight.

The next time Konstantinos and his motley crew came to class I'd pinned a world map to the back wall with a red coloured pin in the UK and a blue one in Greece.

"Where's France, Litza?" I handed her a white pin. Litza wandered up to the map, umm-ed and ahh-ed for about a minute, then stuck it in the correct place.

"And what's the capital...anyone?"

"Paris, obviously *Kyria*." Litza chose to answer. She looked very pleased with herself.

"Well done! Yes, obviously, but be sure to double check your homework in the future for any mistakes." *OK, I'll let the matter drop then. At least she's got it correct.* Taking care not to boast, I then started to reminisce about my worldwide travels.

"Miss, call out the countries you've been to, we'll find them and place a pin on the map" said Konstantinos, taking the initiative for once. Soon the map became an interesting array of colours and I began to see my role not only as a teacher here, but also to help broaden their horizons and stimulate an interest in other cultures. The class was a great success, and I decided to do something similar with the younger children. Bettina and her group chose to pair up to research various countries. By the end of the week, there were a variety of colourful posters on my classroom walls with pictures ranging from Spaniards dancing the flamenco to the mountainous beauty of New Zealand.

While I was popular with the students, I still felt unwelcomed by the other teachers. Although Manos drove me home from work and would often stop by the roadside café to purchase the renowned *spanakopita*, Helena, Eleni and Alexandra still acted cool. I'd tried to initiate discussions with them in the staffroom, but I'd had no joy. They'd smile politely, then Eleni would then stick in her headphones and Helena and Alexandra would pop off to buy a coffee together, never asking if I wanted one.

On the other hand, Mrs Stella was acting much more warmly. She'd occasionally call me into the office to ask my advice about particular students—what did I think of so-and-so and how was so-and-so's behaviour in my class.

Maybe this is why they're funny: she seems to talk to me more than them.

"And Konstantinos, he is behaving himself, no? He knows he's attractive, and I fear his ego gets in the way."

"I'm finding ways to keep them out of mischief." I

smiled at the memory of Konstantinos's face when he discovered his preferred date was Dimitra. I wasn't going to be sycophantic, but Mrs Stella was the most important person for me to get along with—especially as I was living in an apartment in her house. I was enjoying teaching the kids and having Kaliopi as a friend. She certainly made life interesting! I knew I couldn't be liked by everybody, so I was just going to have to stop trying so hard. It was a good principle to live by, but maybe I should also think about applying it to my relationship with Kirsty?

At Kaliopi's insistence, I agreed to join her in Athens on the last weekend of October.

"You have been in my beautiful country for over a month and still have not been to its capital city. An important weekend in Greece's history is coming up, and Athens will be the perfect place to experience it. Besides, you need to get out of this hole of shit. You are becoming like one of *them*, a local."

I smiled. I didn't see the village as a "hole of shit". She might, but I hadn't tired of its rugged mountains and quaint shops yet. But Kaliopi did have a point: I hadn't been to Athens and had no idea what the weekend of 28 October meant in Greek history. What better way to find out than with my Greek friend?

That was how, on Friday night after school, I found myself standing with Kaliopi at the village railway station, waiting for the last train to whisk us to Athens.

"Ah yes, this is an important weekend. Go! I will

cover your remaining class of the day; you need to make that train. Go and learn!" Mrs Stella had been uncharacteristically generous and enthusiastic. I wondered what, exactly, I might learn this weekend?

"We'll be arriving in the capital pretty late, eleven p.m." I said, eyeing the quaint station, complete with its stone cottage railway house with an incongruous-looking thatched roof.

"Don't be silly" snorted Kaliopi, who was wearing what could only described as a clubbing outfit of black high heels, a navy blue sequined skirt, red vest top with a pink rose pinned over the left breast her black jacket only just covered. "You have surely been here long enough to understand that it is not until 1 a.m. that things start—how you say? —'hotting the up' in Greece. But of course," she patted my hand in sympathy, "you have been stuck here in this hole of shit the whole time, so you are turning into a Hillbill."

"Hillbilly," I automatically corrected as I looked down at my jeans, Marks-and-Spencer t-shirt and trainers. I suddenly felt under-dressed and far too plain in comparison. I smiled at my friend's skewed English but, reflecting on my own dress sense of late, I thought: *Maybe I am turning into a hillbill.*

"We will go out straight from the train and meet some of my friends. You will get an education this weekend, my dear, a lesson about our history and a lesson on how genuine Greek people really are—not these hillbills." Kaliopi had a habit of not really paying any attention to the English corrections I made. That— and the fact I was becoming increasingly aware that it was quite rare for me to actually get a word in edgeways around my friend—made me wonder if she ever really listened to me at all.

"Are you like this with everybody?" I asked her.

"Actually, I have complaints from my sisters that I talk too much, is that what you mean? Come to think of it, my other friends tell me the same. Is it true? Do I talk too much? It doesn't mean I don't appreciate your friendship."

I was saved from answering as a growing rumble from the tracks announced the approaching southbound train. We were the only ones on the platform.

"Come along" yelled Kaliopi above the noise of the screeching brakes. She boarded the carriage and held out her hand. "Let us leave this *Railway Children* station for the lights and the action!" Smiling, I allowed myself be swept along by her current high.

"What do you know about *The Railway Children?*"

"I watched it when I was younger, and this station always reminds me of it. Probably the only nice thing about this shit hole."

"Hey! You said it right."

I settled into a big, comfy seat whilst Kaliopi wandered off. *So, not quite the old Soviet-style carriages I'd been anticipating, then,* I thought. The train was more spacious than the trains in the UK, and cheaper given the two-and-a-half-hour journey. Kaliopi tottered back with two steaming cups.

"Coffee for me, and of course, the tea for you."

Ahh, Athens. I drew in a deep breath of air, and started

to cough.

"Oh, I wouldn't do that if I were you," Kaliopi advised. "You're not in the village now. Athens has been labelled as the smokiest city in the world."

"Smoggiest. And what about Beijing?"

"So, I have changed my mind," Kaliopi continued, once again ignoring my correction and question. "We will go to my apartment, get you something else to wear," she gave me the once over "and *then* we shall go out about one a.m. to meet Dimitrios and Nektarios. Oh, and probably Melanthi and anyone else that turns up." I stifled a yawn. *How does she do it? And I didn't start my day until about two p.m...she's been up since 6, probably running too!*

"Come, we need to get the trolley to my apartment. And be careful around here—there are some strange people."

"Stranger than you?" I joked with her. This time she reacted.

"Yes, believe it or not, I am one of the tamer Greeks."

She was right about the strange people: on the way to the trolley, whatever the hell that was, we found ourselves walking through a crowd of young Greeks with black scarves wrapped around their faces, wielding steel baseball bats. Kaliopi cleared a path straight through the middle of them and they parted like the Red Sea.

"Kaliopi!" I hissed. "Shouldn't we cross over to the other side of the road?"

"Eh? Don't mind these idiots," she said, a little too loudly for my liking. "We are the 'right colour.' Just hold your head high and they will leave us alone. Besides, they are probably admiring your English rose complexion, despite your jeans and that awful t-shirt." I was left to ponder the remark about "being the right colour," but decided not to push the matter further. I'd discovered, in my limited time in Greece, that one of its drawbacks was a significant lack of tolerance towards immigration, rather like British attitudes back in the 1950s.

As we stepped through the small gathering, I did indeed notice that they were paying me no attention whatsoever.

"So what exactly are they doing, casually hanging around on the street corner with baseball bats?" I asked her, once we'd passed.

She stopped and turned to face me, causing me to bump into her.

"Rachel, I don't know the workings of the minds of stupid people. We're not in a particularly 'nice' area of Athens, the train station never has been. Maybe they feel they're protecting the area...a Greek vigilante group? If you're that intrigued, go and ask them."

"I think I'll give that a miss, thanks." Despite her frivolousness, I felt safe around Kaliopi. I allowed her to lead.

Suddenly, "Quick, run!" she yelled, grabbing my hand and tugging me into the road.

Oh God, we thought we were safe, but they're after us! I glanced back. But no; they were still just hanging around, some smoking, others chatting, drinking frappes from plastic cups—all looking bored. Up ahead, I saw a yellow "bus" pull up, with antennae on its roof attached to two parallel overhead wires that were dangling over the road. It was towards this that Kaliopi was dragging me.

"Ah, that is better," she sighed after sinking into the seat. "These dashes for the trolley always leave me short of the breath. Now then, we will get you into my flat, re-dress you, and you will be 'as rain as right' as you say in your country."

Ninety minutes later, I found myself sitting in a cosy bar, sipping hot chocolate. I was increasingly enjoying evenings in Greece as I realised the people had a much more civilized approach to a night out: no-one seemed to give a damn that I didn't want an alcoholic drink...there was no pressure. I was squeezed between two of Kaliopi's friends—Nektarios and Dimitrios—having first shoehorned my upper body into what can only be described as a black boob tube. It turned out this was the only item of clothing Kaliopi had that fitted my larger frame, and it went well with my jeans and trainers.

Nektarios was tall, with a strong, square jawline and short-cropped black hair. He wore black cargo trousers and a black t-shirt. He'd nodded at me, but seemed a little moody. Trying to be polite and remembering my students' enquiries into my own black clothes, I asked him if anyone had passed away in his family lately. "What have you been teaching her there in the countryside, Kalipoi?" Nektarios looked at me quizzically. *OK then*, I thought, *it's just his dress sense. Clearly it fits his Mr Darcy image.* I smiled, a little embarrassed, not least because it was rather difficult not to stare at him.

By contrast, Dimitrios was only just slightly taller than Mr Ilias. He wore colourful trousers, a bright purple t-shirt and had the loveliest smile that touched his eyes, in contrast with Nektraias's smouldering moodiness.

Moving on from my comment about black clothing, they started in on my education: the significance of the next day; the 28th of October.

"It's 'Ochi Day'", Nektarios began. "'Ochi' means 'No' in Greek. It's the date in 1940 that our Prime Minister, Ioannis Metaxas, refused Mussolini's ultimatum to surrender to Italy. We entered the Second World War on that day—we said 'OCHI!!' to that asshole," Nektarios finished loudly by raising his fist in the air. *OK then, moody yet passionate,* I concluded.

"Ochi!!" shouted the occupants of several tables around them who'd heard this exchange, again with the raised fist. "Ochi!!" yelled an elderly gentleman, raising his fist as he passed by outside under the open windows of the bar.

"Wow, that day certainly has significance and support around here. Unfortunately kids in our country don't pay much attention to significant historical events. And I'm sorry, I don't know the exact date Britain entered World War Two," I admitted.

"Er… Rachel," said Dimitrios, "I don't want to sound critical of your nation, but you all seem a little apathetic and appear to neither know nor want to learn about important events that shaped your country. This is a shame; it makes your people appear shallow and uneducated, which clearly *you* are not." He finished, beaming that smile of his, dissolving any insult I may have felt.

I thought for a minute and concluded he was right; compared to Greece, at least, we are apathetic about anything political or historical that has helped to shape our present and is important for us to understand. It was another characteristic difference between our nations.

"Don't worry," Dimitrios continued. "Come with us to the Ochi Day Parade tomorrow morning; you'll continue your education with us."

"Oh," groaned Kaliopi. "But it starts so *early*. I need to lie in. Come by my apartment tomorrow morning, collect and take her with you. And you boys, look after Rachel and don't wake me up."

"Now who's being shallow, Kaliopi?" Nektarios jibed, "but OK, we'll do just that," he winked at me and smiled, his face transformed.

Another thing I noted about these two characters—in contrast to my students at school, who didn't speak *bad* English, these two spoke English perfectly. OK, so they were older than my teen class, but I still wanted to know how they'd learned.

"A Masters in English Literature, from Essex University," Nektarios was visibly proud of this fact. "Although," his shoulders slumped, "these days it's hard to get a job in Greece, so I deliver pizza. Such a waste of a degree. But at least I got to experience living in the UK, alas also got to see how much you people seem to want to waste your time going out and getting drunk on the weekends, and you call that living!"

Dimitrios jumped in before I could start protesting—although to be fair, Nektarios had a point and there was really not much to protest about. "I work as a tour guide, so I get to practise my English every day. Also, as you'll see the longer you're here and teaching, the system here in Greece really pushes for people to obtain some form of English language certificate from a young age. It's vital, for a nation that relies on tourism so much."

Sunday dawned bright and early for me, despite having only rolled into bed a few short hours ago. "You can have the bed, I'll sleep on the floor. I don't snore, and I hope you don't either," had been Kaliopi's last words before she fell into a deep sleep.

Hope she's changed the bed sheets—I dread to think what last went on in here, were my last waking thoughts. Now I felt groggy...but also intrigued; I'd get to see how "Ochi Day" would be celebrated.

I have a degree in International Relations, but I knew nothing about Greece. At least this 'Ochi Day' will give me the opportunity to have a more intimate glimpse into Greece's past. I was thoroughly enjoying the brilliant sunshine and bright blue skies Greece offered in plentiful doses, but I was discovering there was far more to this country than initially met the eye. The chance to learn more about it was tempting. *And the chance to not appear so shallow…* I was reminded of Dimitrios's comments last night.

A gentle knock on the door signalled the boys' arrival.

"I'm heading out now," I whispered to a snoring Kaliopi—despite last night's assertions, she actually snored like a train.

Closing the door quietly behind me, I smiled at them both.

"*Pame,* come. Let us take you to Syntagma—Constitution Square—where we will show you what happens on this day" smiled Dimitrios. I marvelled at how wide awake they seemed, until they produced a small Styrofoam cup of Greek coffee. "Kaliopi told me that I wasn't ready for Greek coffee," I said.

"Try it," encouraged Nektarios.

"I made myself a cup at home once, so I know what it tastes like."

"Yes, but try *this* one" Nektarios insisted. Gingerly, I sipped what looked to be a cup of mud. It set my heart rate hammering and snapped my eyes wide open.

"Have you put something else into this?"

They smiled. "No, you're just trying the proper stuff," Dimitrios assured me.

That explains it. They live off this stuff, I concluded, looking at their sparkling eyes. Who needs drugs when Greek coffee's on offer? And Kaliopi was right...I don't think I'll ever be ready for this stuff.

After a trolley ride and a ten-minute walk through streets crowded with people, we arrived in Syntagma Square. Nektarios had purchased three Greek flags to wave at the passing parade. Many people carried nationalistic paraphernalia such as more flags, flag badges and small banners proclaiming "Ochi!"

The square teemed with people. Whole families were there; old ladies displayed banners and children, perched on their fathers' shoulders, waved their flags. At eleven o'clock the military band struck up its march, followed by old soldiers who'd served in the Second World War, who were followed in turn by a selection of schools from the area.

"Do you know who carries the Greek flag at the front of each school's delegation?" Dimitrios pointed to a young girl in a uniform of white shirt and navy blue tie and skirt, who was struggling to carry the huge flag. "It's the most intelligent student in the school of that year. That student has the honour of representing his or her school by carrying the flag in this parade. Every student aspires to be voted the brainiest in order to be awarded this opportunity."

"Yes, but the problem is," Nektarios chimed in, "nowadays the 'brainiest' could be of non-Greek descent."

"Why's that a problem?" I was confused.

"Well, it's not a problem for people like me and Dimitrios. We are open-minded. But a lot of Greeks aren't. You will find, at this time of year, people on television debating the issue. Some claim that non-Greeks shouldn't be allowed to carry the Greek flag—even if one of them happens to be the brightest in school—since they are not true Greeks. We invented the word 'xenophobia.'" Silently I marvelled at how the Greeks got away with being so openly nationalistic, almost racist by my standards.

Were there parades held at home in which a marcher struts in front, proudly waving the Union Jack? I couldn't recall any, and if there were I doubt there'd ever be a televised debate about the multicultural origin of the flag carrier. I couldn't decide whether Greece was excessively celebrating their nationhood, or if the UK was trying too hard to remove any celebration of theirs. Not coming from a county that had ever been occupied, at least in recent history, I doubted I'd fully understand the concept of nationhood and how important it is to its citizens. As if reading my mind, Dimitrios said:

"I'm not making excuses for racist attitudes, but when a country's been occupied as much as this one has, you can understand where they come from, especially the older generation who've lived through a lot."

I watched the excitement on everybody's faces... seeing them come alive at the memory that their country had fought so hard. My history has been a lot easier than that of the people of this nation. We're all forged in the crucible of our nation's history. When I came here I just wanted sunshine and beaches, but there's so much more to discover. Given my different historical upbringing, I wondered about my empathy and my ability to become as excited as the Greeks about such events.

After the parade, we went to eat in a place that resembled a New York City delicatessen that displayed a selection of freshly prepared food and salads: I chose my dish and it was heated and served with a glass of wine and water. I perked up when I saw the homemade desserts on display. As I tucked into a tiramisu, Kaliopi arrived and plonked herself next to us.

"So this is Exarchia—traditionally an 'anarchist' area of Athens where it's thought people from the left meet to 'plot'" she informed me.

"Plot what?"

"You know, to overthrow the government." *No, I don't know!* The concept seemed so far removed from my everyday life that I found it difficult to imagine.

"*So that* explains why there are so many police around here." Every street corner seemed occupied with men clad in navy blue uniforms, *Top Gun* shades and desert boots; they carried riot shields, gas masks, guns and canisters of tear gas.

"Yes, don't be alarmed," said Nektarios. "But also don't think that these are your friendly neighbourhood policemen either, because they aren't," he continued. *Clearly not,* I thought. *Look at their get-up! They look like they're ex-Navy SEALS.* "Don't ask them for directions. They will ask to see your passport and proof of who you are without any reason…just because they can."

"Should I be worried then?" I asked. "I mean, all I'm doing is eating tiramisu, not planning to overthrow the state."

"No," it was Dimitrios' turn, "Nektarios is exaggerating. Although they look scary with their uniforms, I'm sure if you were lost they would help a pretty girl like you."

I wondered what would happen if I weren't so 'pretty?' At least we're not afraid of our police force in the U.K., or more to the point, at least I feel comfortable asking for directions. These guys? They look like they'd relish the chance to stamp on me.

Kaliopi leaned in to polish off the last mouthful of my tiramisu, literally just as I was about to fork it. "Let's take Rachel to the Acropolis, there's more to Athens than military parades."

"Too tired. You go" Nektarios bowed out and told us he was off home to sleep. *Shame, I'd been enjoying his moody "Mr Darcy" presence.*

Two stops on the metro later, we arrived at the Acropolis at about three p.m. Athens only had three metro lines and the trains were quick and clean. The stations were really clean too. I could get used to this civilized way of travelling: elevator-style music playing on the platform, a computer screen displaying the next 3 days' weather forecast, and what was this? The Acropolis metro stop had ancient artefacts housed behind glass displays! No comparison to the London Underground. I voiced my admiration to Kaliopi.

"Yes, but you must realise that the Athens Metro was only built in 2004 for the Olympic Games, so of course it's more modern. You've had your Underground for horse's years."

"Those artefact displays, they're incredible!" I continued. "In London, any such displays would be regularly broken into and/or graffitied."

"Well, you people clearly have no respect for your history," Kaliopi observed flippantly, then announced we'd go to the Acropolis Rocks. "It's at the base of the Parthenon and you get a great view of Athens, as far out as Piraeus."

"I stayed in Piraeus when I first arrived here."

"Never mind, dear." Kaliopi patted my arm, helping me over the marble rocks, trying to find somewhere to sit.

"Beautiful, isn't it?" said Dimitrios after he'd spread his jacket for us to sit on.

"Yes, it is, but there are a number of young teenage couples that should *really* be thinking about getting a room," I said drily as I viewed young teens—about my oldest students' age—cuddled up close, nibbling each other's ears.

"Oh, ignore them" Kaliopi piped up. "They're here all the time. These rocks are famous for young lovers. And it is romantic, with the view and everything, don't you think? But of course, the English: they are so uptight about such things, public displays of this affection," she added. *Ouch—another barb about my nation in the space of half an hour! But spot on.*

"Kaliopi, you realise I'm English and although a lot of the time you're correct, you're not being very nice about my fellow countrymen."

"You're more Greek than I am Rachel, you fit right in here…you'll see in time."

Dimitrios smiled…he was used to Kaliopi's cryptic comments.

Behind us stood the Parthenon, and just beyond that, a flagpole proudly flying a huge Greek flag. Seeing me eyeing this Dimitrios explained, "When Germany finally invaded Greece on 27th April 1941, a German soldier demanded Konstantinos Koukidis, the Guard of the Greek flag here, to hoist the Swastika instead, or be shot. Koukidis took the flag, but when he reached the flagpole, he wrapped himself in the Greek flag and threw himself from the Holy Rock. He would rather kill himself than fly the German flag that represented occupation, and so the Resistance Movement in Greece was born."

I was humbled by such an act of bravery. This country's history of being occupied and being the underdog must be a factor in its desire to literally 'put the flags out' when celebrating a day such as 'Ochi Day.' The history of a country does, indeed, shape its people. I was increasingly impressed by what little history I'd learnt so far. I wasn't quite sure, though, if Greece's history explained Kaliopi's excitable nature.

Descending, we wandered to Plaka, a fashionable tourist area near the Acropolis. We spent a pleasant hour chatting over coffee in the late afternoon sunshine. When the shadows lengthened, Dimitrios gave us both a Greek farewell kiss and hug.

"Come again, and soon. It was lovely to meet an English girl/secret Greek who is actually *interested* in our nation—not just here for the sunshine and alcohol on the islands!" I smiled, pleased that I'd managed to scrape beneath the surface and meet some lovely people—and also pleased I'd not voiced my original attraction to Greece.

We headed back to clean up Kaliopi's apartment, gather our belongings and return to the village.

"We'll meet my friends again, don't worry, and probably Melanthi next time too, I think she must have been away this weekend," said Kaliopi as we made our way to the railway station. As the train pulled in to return us to our weekday realities, I noticed a subdued mood had shrouded my friend.

"You know how much I hate the village, with its farmers who don't clean under their fingernails and shout at me when they come into the bank where I work. Athens is my home and I love her, but I can't get a job there unless my bank transfers me. They won't do that unless there is a vacancy. And as nobody wants to work in the hole of shit provinces, I am stuck there for the time being!"

"At least you have me," I offered as consolation.

"Yes, I have you" she visibly brightened. *"Pame, pame, katze kato;* Come, come and sit down" Kaliopi patted the seat next to her.

The train pulled away and I smiled down at Kaliopi who'd promptly fallen asleep on my shoulder and started to snore again, mouth ajar and dribbling ever so slightly.

Chapter 7

School continued. The same issues with Dimitra and Konstantinos recurred, and I found myself having to dream up ever more innovative ways of dealing with them. One day, however, things took a turn in the opposite direction. I stumbled across them in a street near the school—kissing. "Ahem," I cleared my throat.

"Ah, *Kyria* Rachel." Konstantinos didn't look at all embarrassed. In fact he seemed rather pleased with himself. "Dimitra has a problem with her family."

"And you're helping her how, exactly?" Blushing, Dimitra glanced away. "Besides, I thought you hated each other."

"Love ... hate, is this not the same thing?" Konstantinos asked. *God, so astute and cynical at such a young age.*

"Regardless," I continued, "we're not here to discuss love. You have class and should be in Mr Manos's room right about...now" I peered at my watch. I pushed them on their way, but not without a last plea from this Greek Romeo and Juliet.

"*Please* don't tell Mrs Stella you found us."

I pretended to ponder this for a minute. "Hmm, well ...." I trailed off, leaving the sentence unfinished.

"Oh *Kyria*, we will be quiet in class from now on,"

offered Dimitra.

"And I'll buy you a coffee," added Konstantinos, winking at me. This thing with Dimitra was inflating his ego more than usual.

"Konstantinos, winking at your teacher isn't really appropriate. Save that for Dimitra." *Ah, that got him.* He looked away, embarrassed. "But," I continued more gently, "I'll take you up on that offer of a drink at the end of the school year—thanks." They beamed as they headed off to class hand in hand, leaving me to ponder the complexities of teenage strife.

Not long after Ochi Day, another holiday came along. Although not an official public holiday, the schools didn't open on 17th November and luckily for me, it fell on a Monday.

It was a perfect opportunity for a long weekend, and another chance to educate myself about significant dates in modern Greek history. I felt proud of myself: wanting to know more about my host country rather than just taking it at face value. Kaliopi and I got up early on the Saturday and boarded the coach for Athens.

"I've had enough of trains," she stated. I could understand why: from my point of view, although the train was faster and cheap, the village station was at least twenty minutes out of town. My only experience of the train was the time I went to Athens for the weekend and whilst it was quaint, it was quite scary at night and early morning…not because of potential crime—more because of its isolated location. The station was pretty sinister, especially with the hooting owls and the screeching. *I hope they're foxes and not wolves—or maybe that's my overactive imagination again.* Having travelled by bus a short distance from school occasionally, I knew what to expect: people unwilling to move their bags from the window seat. But this time it wouldn't be an issue with the two of us travelling; we picked an empty row together.

"What about the tickets?" I asked as we sat down. "Shouldn't we have bought them beforehand at the bus station?" We'd boarded outside a small café two stops away from the main village terminus.

"Don't worry," replied Kaliopi. "The conductor will come and take your money. Get it ready—he doesn't like to wait." He was ambling down the aisle, collecting everyone's fare. Luckily we both had the exact change—buying bread the previous week had taught me how much Greeks loathe making change, and often round up or down to the nearest five cents to avoid giving and receiving the pesky one and two cent coins. When he reached us, I couldn't help noticing his right pinkie fingernail—it was about a centimetre long. Trying not to stare, I pointed it out to Kaliopi once he'd passed.

"Oh, that. You see? You can tell he's from a village. It's something to do with tradition in these parts, although I suspect it has more to do with nose-picking" came her laconic reply.

I smiled, leaned back in the cushioned seat and took in the scenery: wind farms high above the road on surrounding mountains; small roadside taverns; people bent over picking cotton in the fields. For ninety minutes we rolled through the picturesque landscape, stopping once or twice in small towns to collect more passengers. Then the scenery changed: more cars and built-up areas. Finally it was obvious we were approaching Athens: apartment blocks five or six stories high with green awnings shading balconies and CDs dangling from string to scare off the pigeons.

It was still early when we arrived.

"Let's go back to my apartment for a little more sleep" Kaliopi suggested, "before we venture out." Once again she gave me the bed; once again she commented that she hoped I wouldn't snore like last time. I couldn't help wondering who'd been in here last and if she'd changed the sheets. I didn't have the heart to ask her, or to tell her that she was the one who rivalled a freight train. We awoke near midday, refreshed but hungry.

"Come, there's nothing here to eat. Let's go and grab some *gyros*," Kaliopi suggested. Gyros turned out to be strips of pork or chicken, freshly made chips ("*patates*" fried in olive oil), salad and mayonnaise or *tzatziki*—the traditional Greek dip of yogurt, cucumber, lemon juice and lots of garlic—all bundled together in a thick pita wrap. Having skipped breakfast that morning, I was ravenous. This was the sort of fare the cafés in the village sold all the time, but I hadn't actually tried one yet. *I could get to like Greek fast food.* Appetites finally sated, we lounged outside the small neighbourhood café in the November sun alongside the locals. Kaliopi's neighbourhood wasn't in a touristy section of Athens, so I had the opportunity to watch her neighbours go about their day, uninterrupted by streams of foreigners. Her apartment fronted onto a small square with a domed church and at a pavement table in the *kafinion* opposite us sat a table of four elderly men, playing *tavli*, occasionally shouting at each other and slapping each other on the back. A cluster of young boys and a couple of girls kicked a ball to each other while their mothers sat on the bench seat fixed around the monkey puzzle tree dominating the centre of the square.

"We will meet my friends again later." She licked the last of the *tzatziki* from her fingers. "Come, I need fruits and there is a farmer's market somewhere around here on a Saturday."

Indeed there was—we just had to follow the cries of the stallholders and follow the elderly ladies dragging large shopping trolleys to find it only three streets away. I picked out two red apples and tried to pay, only to be looked at by the stallholder as if I'd insulted him. He waved me away with a flick of his hand. *"Dyo evro Copella, tipota!"* he smiled.

"It's because you only want two items," Kaliopi clarified. "He's just told you two euros is nothing to him…if you'd bought more, he would have charged you." Impressed by this act of kindness, I insisted that Kaliopi buy the salad vegetables from him. Feta cheese and meat from the local butchers completed our shopping for our evening meal and we made our way back to the apartment. It was nice to see that as well as supermarkets, it was possible to still find local shops in the capital city, and not just the village.

Kaliopi had made the decision earlier that we wouldn't be going out that evening; instead she'd invited 'a couple of friends over.' A couple of Kaliopi's friends turned out to be Melanthi, Nektarios, Dimitrios, Dimitrios's sister Maria, Nektarios's cousin Evangelia, her boyfriend Menelaos and Menelaos's dentist (of all people!), Eleni. I was left reeling in confusion with the introductions as they all trooped in at nine o'clock, kissing each other on both cheeks and welcoming me in a similar vein. *Hold on, is Evangelia the dentist and Eleni Nektarios's cousin?* Still, there were definitely more than "a couple of friends." I was bursting to know how the dentist fitted into the circle, but an enquiry to Nektarios about this merely resulted in his asking,

"Which one is the dentist again? Ask Menelaos, he's the one who brought her." Kaliopi, not having been introduced to the dentist nor Menelaos before that night either, didn't seem to mind and busied herself pulling pillows from the bed.

"You'll have to sit here, Eleni… Evangelia… Maria—whoever," she threw the pillows onto the floor. "*Katze, katze,* sit, sit. I am preparing *stifado* with salad." That explained the smell wafting from the kitchen during the afternoon. I'd heard of this hearty winter meat dish: beef stew with small onions, vinegar, red wine, and cinnamon. But Kaliopi was preparing hers with rabbit— which would be a first for me.

"I'm Melanthi, we didn't meet last time, I was away working in Dubai," one of the girls extended her hand and shook mine formally, but with a smile. "I work for a major hotel chain in marketing and I get to travel a lot. Don't let Kaliopi overwhelm you." She leant forward confidentially, "she's a lovely person with a very kind heart. I've known her for many years."

"Yes, she's really taken me under her wing in the short time I've got to know her," I smiled as Kaliopi came back into the room, carrying a pot full of steaming stew.

We all tucked into the *stifado* and salad, comple-
mented by a bottle of red wine. I found that rabbit didn't
taste all that different from beef, and as I settled back and
allowed the good-natured arguing to manifest around
me, and ducking away from Kaliopi's flying fork as she
rammed home a point, I found myself warming to the
idea of enjoying life without all the need for advanced
planning. So far in Greece, the times I'd most enjoyed
had evolved spontaneously.

*I need to allow myself to let go even more, to go
with the flow,* I thought. *Hell, I've managed well with
the time keeping issue...* My thoughts were interrupted
as a piece of meat flew onto my plate from Nektarios's fork as he rallied against Kaliopi's argument. Life
in Greece seems to consist of constantly fielding curve-
balls (and flying meat). I smiled at Kaliopi, still arguing
and jabbing her fork in the direction of Nektarios and his
cousin, Evangelia. He glanced over at me and winked.
"We let her run out of the steam when she's like this,"
he attempted the English idiom with little error. "She's
complaining about the village...again." He shrugged his
shoulders.

"We keep telling her to be patient, a job will come
up in Athens soon, and she has you now...this is good,
no?" Melanthi joined in.

"Yes, it is good, for the both of us," I replied.

I left them to it at three o'clock on Sunday morning
and retired to the bedroom, leaving Kaliopi continuing
her rant in the sitting room with Dimitrios, whose sister
had long departed. I closed my eyes, thinking about how
people in Greece didn't feel compelled to leave a social

gathering with the people they came with. It was all very relaxed. In fact, when Menelaos had left earlier, leaving his dentist friend deep in conversation with Nektarios, he'd stated he didn't want to pay for a taxi, and it was too late for public transport. Leaning out of Kaliopi's third-floor balcony, I'd witnessed him chatting with a twenty-four-hour pizza delivery motorbike man whom he'd flagged down in the street. After a moment, he turned back and yelled up, "Don't worry about me, I'm getting a lift home. *Kali nichta all!*"

We slept until early afternoon on Sunday, and then eventually made our way to Plaka. We took our time meandering through the flea market that offered everything from old books and coins to Nike running shoes and army paraphernalia. Needing to rest, we stopped at another *gyros* outlet, and as we sat outside and ate, I marvelled at how warm it was for November—about 18 degrees —it was still jeans and t-shirt weather.

"So, what's the plan for tomorrow?" I took a bite of my chicken *gyros*.

"I will take you to the university, where you will learn another part of our history," replied Kaliopi, solemn for once.

Greece was turning out to be so much more than just a job in the sun.

Bright and early Monday morning, I was awakened by Kaliopi shaking me, a cup of strong Greek coffee in her hand.

"Drink this, get up and get ready," she ordered.

"So I'm ready for Greek coffee now, am I?"

"We must get going! You have a lot to learn today."
I didn't press for answers—mostly because I wanted it
to remain a surprise, but also because I was still so damn
tired at—what was this—eight thirty on my day off? I
groaned as I rolled over and placed the coffee on the
side table. I heard footsteps padding out of the room,
followed by sounds of the shower running and Kaliopi
singing at full blast, I heaved myself out of bed and
walked out onto the balcony. Dodging a hanging CD, I
poured the coffee into the nearest aloe vera plant. I didn't
want to offend her, yet my last experience with Greek
coffee with the boys left me assured that its caffeine jolt
would leave me jittery and headachy all day. Judging by
the state of this plant, I wondered if Kaliopi's various
male visitors also had the same idea.

We finally left the house around ten o'clock.—after
I'd showered with what little hot water Kaliopi had left
me, and after she'd dosed herself with coffee and a cigarette on the balcony. *I love Kaliopi, I really do. But why
wake me at 8:30am when we leave at 10?* I grumbled
away to myself. I wasn't in the best of moods. Maybe I
should've drunk the coffee after all.

As we walked to the trolley I noticed many other
people heading in the same direction. Most carried
banners.

"Oh look, another parade like Ochi Day! Will we
see schoolchildren carrying the flag again?" I asked.
Now we were outside I felt better, less moody. I'd not
noticed the tear gas masks carried by most people and
also failed to notice Kaliopi's 'look.'

"Dear girl," Kaliopi replied, patting me on the

shoulders. "You have no clue, do you? It is good that you are coming today. But I will keep you away from trouble, don't worry." This last sentence Kaliopi mumbled, but loudly enough for me to hear it. Experience told me to trust her, and besides, I was too busy enjoying what I perceived to be the high spirits of everyone around me.

Complete strangers were chatting, as they had on my first Athens trolley ride. I began to warm to Athens... it was a city in which you could never feel truly alone— someone was always willing to talk to you. As a traveller, I felt quite safe here.

"Here we are, the Polytechnic," announced Kaliopi, assuming tour guide status. "*Ela,* come." We left the trolley, along with half the other passengers who disappeared up the street in the direction of the city centre.

"We are standing at the gates where students were killed by a military tank that crashed into the grounds in the early morning of 17 November 1973," began Kaliopi. I must have looked stricken because Kaliopi reached out and patted my hand. She sighed. "You are from a country that has never been oppressed and subjugated; you are from a different thought process entirely. Therefore it must be hard for you to understand what we have suffered in this beautiful land throughout our history."

"You'd better tell me more," I felt deflated from my earlier jubilation.

"Come into the building. They show an old film clip from a Dutch journalist who was secretly filming the whole episode from across the street." She pointed to a beautiful colonial-style, rundown building, with a similar façade to many of the other neglected buildings I'd seen in Athens. This one used to be a hotel.

Entering the Polytechnic we made our way into a room whose walls were lined with pictures of students who had lost their lives that day. Many people were there, looking at the projector screen. I squeezed into the back, and at last the fuzzy footage sprang to life. A tank was advancing towards the Polytechnic main gates, from which students were hanging.

Kaliopi, eyes welling with tears, explained "One of the students pleaded with the soldiers to disobey the military order to do whatever possible to stop the student protests. He called them 'Brothers in Arms'. He refused to jump from the gate and as it got nearer, he started to sing the National Anthem. Look what happens next."

The tank then crashed into the gate: the screen went blank and the sound stopped. The spectators in the room fell silent as well. The footage was rewound to be replayed for the next batch of visitors. No one made a noise—old people remembering and young people reflecting. It was a good five minutes before we felt ready to leave. Kaliopi was wiping her eyes, smudging her mascara. Kaliopi's family had been directly involved— her parents had grown up under this dreadful military regime. Therefore she'd no doubt frequently heard tales told about this era and seen the effects of the suffering first hand.

After regaining her composure, Kaliopi said "Come, let's go for coffee and I will fill you in a little more." And sitting in a quiet end of town, away from Exarchia and the brewing troubles, Kaliopi gave me a history lesson I'd never forget.

"Since 1967, Greece had been under military dictatorship. Their practices included forcing "subversive" youths to join the army; imprisoning, torturing and exiling people based on their political beliefs; abolishing civil rights and getting rid of political parties. The *junta* basically wanted to control every aspect of our social and political lives. 17th November 1973 finally saw the students have enough and take control. They went on strike, staged a sit-in in the university grounds..."

"What's a 'sit-in'?" I interrupted, not wanting to misunderstand a thing.

"The students stayed in the grounds, locked the gates and refused to move. They transmitted radio broadcasts across the city and people took to the streets in support in their thousands, until in a panic the military received orders from their leader, Papadopoulos, to take action." Taking a sip of her coffee, Kaliopi paused to light a cigarette.

"And this action involved the tanks," I concluded.

"Yes, what you've just witnessed in that room. Of course, officially they say that no lives were lost that day, and there is still dispute over what is the "truth." But you saw that film [no video back then, surely?] foot. We saw what happened."

Footage, film footage, I thought, but I felt it unnecessary to correct her right at that moment.

"But of course, there is always a silver seam to every cloud" Kaliopi smiled for the first time that day. "All schools and universities in Greece are now a police-free areas, out of respect for what happened both on 17th November and throughout the junta era."

"But what if a crime happens on campus?" this

was my first and obvious thought.

"The police have to be *invited*, this is the point." Kaliopi jabbed her index finger on the table, "they cannot just turn up. Later on today," she continued, "there will be a parade in remembrance of 17th November, but not like the parade you saw back in October. People mistrust the police and anything to do with authority here, for reasons you have just witnessed. So always this 'parade' turns nasty, and people provoke the police, or maybe the police provoke the people—I am never really sure which comes first. It is a—how you say?—'egg with chicken' situation. Then a bottle or Molotov is thrown, the police throw tear gas and the whole thing becomes chaotic. That is why we are keeping away from the centre, and why you should not so innocently smile at the people with banners." I must have looked worried as Kaliopi patted me affectionately, "Don't worry, we'll return to my flat, grab our things, and head back to the village."

Within an hour and a half, we were sitting on the bus, bound for home. "If you have any questions about this day, ask." Kaliopi offered. Plenty swam around in my head: Where does a dictator come from? How do they gain and keep power? And why are we unaware of this period of time in Greece's history? Dad must have known about these things, so how come I didn't? And why did we only ever concentrate on World War II and the wives of King Henry VIII in school history lessons, and not about something so recent that took place within Europe? My thoughts were interrupted when the bus driver turned up his radio, the passengers talking to each other in the weary way of the cynical.

"What's going on?"

"The usual. Nothing out of the ordinary. It's just started, that's all. The first bottle has been thrown, and it is starting to get ugly. And only fifteen minutes into their march," sighed Kaliopi. "Sometimes I wonder if people will ever learn. How do they expect to win respect and instil change if they resort to the anarchy?"

Eventually the bus driver turned off the radio, tired of all the doom and gloom. As we pulled into the village and got off the bus outside the café, Kaliopi hugged me hard and went her own way. I dragged myself up the hill and opened the gate to my flat, looking forward to a rest after an emotional day. Two of the old lady from next door's cats sat on the doorstep, offering me a welcoming meow. As I bent down to scratch them behind the ears, Mrs Stella emerged from her apartment above. *Has she been waiting and watching for my return? God, surely not!* A quick glance at my watch showed nine p.m., not late by Greek standards.

"So, did you learn a little more about Greek history this weekend?" she asked, coming up behind me and helping me to open the door. "Shoo!" she hissed at the cats at the same time. "Do not go encouraging them, they will only want feeding."

"Yes, I never knew about the junta. I assumed it was only South America and Spain that had suffered such regimes."

Mrs Stella pushed the door open to allow me to cross the threshold.

"Greece's history is littered with takeovers, trage-dies, and censorship. But you will come to learn this over time. Off you go to bed—you must be tired. If you are hungry I will tell my husband to bring you some chicken and rice we had for our dinner. Would you like some?"

I hadn't realised just how hungry I was, so I grate-fully accepted. It was an interesting choice of verb: *'tell'* my husband, not 'ask.' But it was kind of her to offer food. I flipped on the TV, hoping to find a mind-numbing film that could help me switch off after the rather gruel-ling day. Most of the channels were filled with either the same footage I'd seen at the university, or scenes of today's chaos in the city. I eventually found an old episode of a popular American sitcom. Sitting upright in bed and munching on the chicken dish, I laughed at the infamous weather-girl who came on during the break; she delivered her forecasts clad in short clothing and in such a suggestive manner that even men found her funny instead of sexy.

"Oh good grief," I mumbled, placing my finished plate on the floor and rolling over in bed. According to Kaliopi, the weather girl was an intelligent young lady with a degree in economics. *Well, she certainly is the clever one here. She's getting paid well to look like that on TV. Clearly I'm in the wrong profession!* I had to admit, however, that people might actually pay me NOT to pose in a bikini on national television.

I drifted into an uneasy sleep in which I dreamt I was at a demonstration, dressed in a bikini, running away from baton-wielding policemen in aviator shades, trying to persuade them that my forecast of sunshine and showers had been correct.

Winter

Chapter 8

At school, the topic of Konstantinos and Dimitra was on everybody's lips. They had now fallen out again. Konstantinos had been caught with Litza, the intelligent *copella* I'd encountered on my first day. I kept her behind after class to ask about this development.

"Litza, you are an intelligent girl. Why are you becoming involved in a love triangle with Konstantinos and Dimitra?" Litza gazed at me with eyes that at first seemed to beg me not to take this conversation further, but then her expression turned to confusion.

"What is this triangle of love you talk about?"

"Well, in Greece you have many tragedies about love, with many people falling for one person," I replied. "So the concept of a love triangle should be easy for you to understand. Just don't get into something you can't handle." Litsa gave me an unhappy nod and trotted off, glancing behind her as she went. Konstantinos was waiting for her at the door and I just caught her whispering to him: "*Kyria* Rachel thinks that love can be understood through mathematics and trigonometry." I smiled and pretended not to hear as I realised this was for my benefit—why else speak to him in English?

I missed Kaliopi at the weekends. Because of her feelings about the village she would, more often than not, escape to Athens on Friday night, returning by train early on Monday morning to go straight to work. I found these times best for exploring the village: the remains of a small castle, the enjoyable—albeit rigorous—walk to a church set into the hillside and the amphitheatre that Kaliopi assured me was no longer used for plays. "In a place like this, are you kidding? That would mean these people were actually cultured. They aren't, as I keep telling you." I was used to her barbs about the village by now and had learnt to let her comments float over my head.

But there was only so much exploring of the village I could do. "Come with me to Athens," she encouraged when I admitted I missed her company.

"I wish I could, but not every weekend...it's not possible. I have student essays to mark and lessons to plan, sorry."

One weekend in December, however, Kaliopi decided it was time to educate me again, therefore she returned to the village on a Saturday night.

I was watching the Greek version of "Pop Idol" when I heard a rap at the window. Thinking it was Mrs Stella, I turned the TV down, the light off and pretended to be asleep... I didn't want to deal with anything she might have to say, particularly if it was work-related. The disadvantage of living in the basement of your boss's property was that you could never tell with Mrs Stella—she might be coming down to tell me she'd decided to stage a Shakespearean play at school and wanted me to direct it, or she might be bringing me a plate of chicken. The knocking grew louder and more insistent until I heard a familiar voice; "I know you're in there. Are you hiding from me?"

"No, no!" I scrambled to let Kaliopi in. "I didn't expect it'd be you. Why're you back so early?" But Kaliopi was momentarily distracted. She was eyeing my little flat and shaking her head.

"You see? A hole of shit. Your boss must have lots of money, and yet she doesn't have the decency to furnish the place properly for you. I bet you her place is better furnished, *eh*?"

"Let's not focus on that, *eh*?" I repeated the very Greek ending of the sentence. Deep inside, I'd been thinking similar thoughts—but despite her demeanour, I felt a strange sort of loyalty towards Mrs Stella.

"Anyway," Kaliopi shook her head as if to clear it of the image in front of her, "I had a few days off work, so I met an Italian acquaintance on his yacht. We sailed for one day, but he couldn't satisfy me, so I slapped him. He yelled 'No-one, not even my mother or sister has slapped me!' and I was afraid he'd throw me out of that round window thing in his boat, so I jumped from his yacht in Santorini and flew back to Athens." I was familiar with Kaliopi's antics by now, but even this escapade gobsmacked me. She continued… "So I've come back early to continue your education. Tomorrow I am taking you to Delphi. Go to bed now because we will take the early bus. It is only a forty-five minute ride, so a day trip is enough."

"Kaliopi, that 'round window' thing is a porthole, and as my friend I want to tell you that I really think you should pick your 'acquaintances' more carefully!" But she was backing out through the door already, glancing around her as if fearing that she might catch something nasty from my 'hole of shit' flat if she stayed longer. I was left with an image of her being thrown through a porthole into the Aegean Sea. This girl was better than a soap opera.

Early the next morning I walked to the bus stop, dressed warmly for the winter weather. Stomping my feet and attempting to blow smoke rings with the clouds my exhalations formed, I waited moodily for my friend. I realised why I love teaching in the afternoons and evenings; I really am not a morning person. At last Kaliopi waltzed up at exactly the right moment for the bus to arrive.

Seeing my grumpy face, she commented, "It's not my fault you are British and always on time. And besides," she looked at me, "what is wrong with you? You are usually, how you say, 'beat-up'?"

"Upbeat," I corrected her, the coldness of my mood starting to defrost in the warm bus. "I'm just not used to early morning rises, especially when it's so cold. Who'd've thought Greece could get so cold in the winter?"

"Yes it does, and you're in the mountains now. You see? It's not sunshine and warmth all year round, but certainly more sunshine at least than your place. This early start will be worth it," Kaliopi said. "Look, we're heading up into the mountains now." We wound up narrow roads and then onto the two-lane highway towards Delphi. The view grew more and more glorious the higher we ascended: steep ravines and drops on either side making me feel a little nervous, log cabins set into the hillside and the occasional goat here and there. It felt more like Switzerland.

After traversing a particularly difficult stretch of mountain road *(God, please let us arrive safely! I promise I'll be nicer in the mornings to everybody)* and passing through the après-ski village of Arachova, known as the "Mykonos" of the winter months due to its clubbing scene and party atmosphere, the bus pulled into the village of Delphi. We disembarked and I looked around. There were the usual tourist shops but also smaller shops of the sort I was used to seeing in the village. One butcher shop was aptly named "Meat Market." I smiled; I doubted if any clubbing or picking up of the opposite sex went on there after hours—but if this shop was in Arachova, then maybe...

Kaliopi gave me a gentle shove in the direction of the Oracle of Delphi archaeological site. "We've plenty of time to look at the town later, when we're hungry and in need of a fill up," she took a cigarette from her handbag.

"Let's go and visit the site first. Besides," she squinted at the clouds tumbling in from the coast, "it looks like rain later."

Delphi was remarkably quiet, but it was the off-season and most of the tourists would be staying in Arachova. We wandered up to the entrance with Kaliopi chattering away. "Did you know that Delphi is considered the Navel of the Earth?" she asked.

"But why? Delphi's nowhere near the sea."

"No!" Kaliopi rolled her eyes and pointed to her stomach. *"This* navel! Good grief, you are an English teacher and you can't tell the difference?"

"Not without seeing it written down," I said in my defence, although it made more sense when I considered it.

"Anyway, a dragon called Pythia lived here and guarded the Navel, or Centre, until the God Apollo destroyed the dragon to make this place his own. Every four years since 586BC, athletes from all over Greece have come to Delphi to compete in the Pythian Games. These Games are just one such example of how the Olympic Games developed...the world has no idea just how much it owes to us Greeks..." She was wandering off into one of her glazed far-away monologues. "Now, look at the view." Kaliopi snapped back to the present. I turned, not realising quite how high we'd climbed whilst discussing local history. The view was gorgeous. The ancient theatre was set against a backdrop of mountains and pines. We carried on up the path in front of us, which took us to the old Pythian Games stadium, situated at the top of the archaeological site where pine trees whispered their welcome. The stadium was shaped like a smaller version of the Olympic Stadium in Athens. We found a flat rock and sat in companionable silence, taking in the surroundings. There was not a soul in sight.

"I thought Gods were supposed to be good people. Why did he go and slay that dragon?" I said after a while.

"Why did your St. George slay that dragon back in the past?" Kaliopi countered.

"From what I remember of the story, the dragon was trying to kill the princess."

"There you go then, I guess all dragons are bad... who knows? Anyway, we better get going." Kaliopi motioned with her head toward the clouds that were moving towards us from the seaside village of Galaxidi that could be seen in the far distance. "Besides, I'm hungry now." Reluctantly I rose and we started walking down. It had been really peaceful amongst the pine trees, soaked in ancient history and the view so unhindered, being able to see as far away as a small coastal town, 15km away.

Sitting in a *taverna* with a covered balcony overlooking the pine clad valleys far below, we ordered various small dishes: *mezze* including small fried potato and courgette croquettes; *tzatziki*; Greek salad and a pork chop each.

"Simple food is the best, eh?" said Kaliopi, squeezing a liberal dose of fresh lemon over her chop. "So, how do you like your day so far?" I hadn't said too much, content to let Kaliopi once again do the talking, allowing myself to absorb and learn. And she'd been correct about the storm—it was starting to rain; waiters were frantically clearing the few outside tables and bringing them in. As the first heavy drops fell, accompanied by a flash of lightning, I snuggled back into my bench seat after polishing off the chop and nursed an after-dinner mug of hot chocolate.

"It's not just Delphi, Kaliopi, it's everything I've experienced so far, meeting you and your friends...taking in Ochi Day and 17th November. In only two months I've learned more history than I could ever have done at school, although they don't look at Greek history in UK schools generally. Today's been magical as well, look at this scenery!"

Kaliopi beamed; proud I'd complimented her country. "Greece is waving her magic wand over you.

I am glad you are not so British. You are not like those people who only visit our islands once a year and go crazy stupid *malakas* drunk. You have style and class. You are a lady. As I've said before, you have the Greek hidden in you." A compliment from Kaliopi was a compliment indeed as she rarely held back her feelings—which could be a blessing or a curse. She was genuinely pleased I'd had a good day and this was important, especially since I recognised that she'd sacrificed a valuable weekend in Athens to be with me and not the latest male 'friend.'

"Come, let us test how truly Greek you are by seeing how you board the bus. You may need to dismiss your English politeness for a bit." We had to wait outside in the rain for our bus back to the village. Not quite understanding what she meant, I dismissed her comment, but all too soon it became clear. Out of nowhere surged a sea of people, mostly old and all barging and fighting in their attempt to board first. Wielding whatever weapons were at hand (umbrellas, elbows, handbags), they pummelled us to the back of the queue. As a result, when it was our turn to board the bus was full.

"Great!" Kaliopi yelled as the driver waved us off and closed his doors. "Now we have to wait for the next one...in another hour!" she rounded off her anger by giving the driver a palm-splayed hand signal.

"At least it's stopped raining," I offered, shouldering some of the responsibility for being stranded. *Maybe I hadn't been 'Greek' enough and should have pushed and shoved to the front.* "And what does this mean?" I copied Kaliopi's gesture.

"Do *not* do that to my face! It is the Greek *mountza*, the worst insult you can ever give anyone. It's the equivalent of saying to someone you want to rub excrement in their face."

I gasped. "Good job the bus driver didn't see you."

No, I certainly did *not* want to do that to my friend, yet was a little taken aback that Kaliopi had felt so strongly about missing the bus.

"Relax," she almost immediately simmered down, "It's sort of like you people extending your middle finger."

And that's another thing about this country: one minute it's like the end of the world, the next everything's OK. It's like dealing with a manic depressive: you never know what to expect. I remembered my first morning in Piraeus, seeing the old men seemingly arguing then making up in the street. Kaliopi was just an extreme example of this.

Not wanting to lose the opportunity to board the last bus and run the risk, this time, of Kaliopi getting into a full blown argument with the bus driver, (although that could have been interesting) we decided to wait near the bus stop rather than risk sitting in a café. We wiped the worst of the rain off a large boulder then plonked ourselves down on it. The rain had cast a different glow over the area, and it positively glistened. I became caught up in the scenery and serenity of the place, already forgetting the stress of earlier, and we'd barely exchanged a word when we heard the distant rumbling of the approaching bus.

"Right," I mumbled, jumping up in preparation for battle with the oldies. "Let's get ready,"

Kaliopi grinned, "*Now* you are turning into a true Greek."

"I just don't want you to be in a position where you have to make that hand signal again."

As the bus pulled up, I glanced around for old people to appear out of cracks and crevices, ready to push us out of the way. But this time the bus was half-empty and the only others boarding were a Japanese couple who had also missed the previous bus.

Disappointed that I hadn't had the chance to do battle, yet secretly relieved (the old people held back nothing, and things might have turned nasty), we shuffled to the back, sat down and fell into a contented doze.

Chapter 9

As winter continued its descent upon the village, the days and evenings became even colder. I should've done my research and not overlooked the fact that Greece still gets cold in the winter, despite its Southern European location. As Kaliopi had pointed out, I was living in a Greek village, nestled in the mountains, in the middle of nowhere. Luckily I'd packed one polo neck jumper. I could layer the rest of my clothes, and I vowed to go warm-clothes shopping with Kaliopi when I was next in Athens. My little semi-basement flat, though criticised by all those who crossed its threshold—which admittedly had only been Kaliopi so far—was surprisingly warm and snug. The neighbour's cats didn't seem to mind huddling in the doorway either.

At this time of year it was dark by 5:30 p.m. and as my classes started at four, my garden classroom would only get an hour and a half of sun-dappled light.

"Miss, we don't eat the salad. Now we eat the *stifado* and the chicken because of the cold," Bettina told me one December day. "I hate the salad anyway," she said, twisting her face in disgust, "and my *yiayia* [Grandma] makes it the good."

The teenagers seemed visibly depressed by the shortened days. Even the usually cheeky Konstantinos couldn't be chided out of his dark mood, so I gave them a break from routine and the exam syllabus by constructing a unique Christmas lesson.

I Googled "Christmas traditions from around the world" and then discussed these in class. I was determined to continue their education of traditions outside of their own.

The project work involving the world map seemed to work, let's give this a try.

"Did you know that on 24th December, Finnish people go to mass as they do in Greece, but then they visit a sauna and for lunch eat porridge containing a hidden almond? The person who discovers this nut has to then sing a carol" I started.

"Miss, what person has a fin?" enquired Bettina, wide eyed. The rest giggled, images of humans with a fin and tail no doubt swimming in front of their eyes.

"Well, a fictional mermaid for a start, but Finnish is the name given to people who live in Finland. Like you, you are Greek because you live in…"

"*Greece*," the class shouted.

"Where's Finland, anyone?" I didn't really expect anyone to know, so it didn't surprise me when no-one offered an answer.

"Here you are, all the way up here." I let the students decide which colour pin to stick in the world map over the country of Finland.

"If it has the snow, we need a white pin" said Bettina "Does it have the snow, *Kyria*?" I smiled at her use of imagination.

"Yes it does, it has *snow*—no need to use the definite article. It also has log cabins in the woods and husky dogs."

Glad of a break from routine, the students visibly warmed to this lesson change. I produced a different activity for the teenagers: by placing fictitious names of people from various countries in Konstantinos's baseball cap, each student was to write a letter to his or her new pen pal, describing their own Greek Christmas traditions.

They seemed to enjoy the writing exercise as well, and definitely appreciated a move away from exam focus.

"*Kyria*, won't Mrs Stella be angry with you? We're not doing anything like this with our other teachers," Dimitra and her classmates were referring to my maverick actions.

That's because they're shit scared of their boss, I thought. "Don't you worry about Mrs Stella," I replied, although I too had wondered how she'd take this, given that she never wanted to lose control of what went on in her school.

"Ah, Miss Rachel," she cornered me that night while I was waiting for Manos to finish up so I could get my usual lift. "What's this about a Christmas lesson? The students have exams soon and it is best to continue with the syllabus, don't you think?" I saw Konstantinos pull a sympathetic face for me behind her back. He raised both his hands with his fingers crossed, offering me support. I realised Mrs Stella had made a statement, not actually asked me a question. She gave a tight smile and made to move off. Clearly the conversation was over for her. I took a deep breath:

"Actually, they're producing some excellent ideas through this particular lesson," I started. "This is going beyond English language acquisition; they're learning to think for themselves, critical thinking skills. Essential for developing ideas in an exam situation wouldn't you think?" I smiled sweetly, pleased with myself at having deliberately picked impressive phrases such as 'language acquisition' and 'critical thinking skills.' And besides, I was right—they were acquiring these skills. "Not to mention broadening their horizons with knowledge of other cultures, all through the medium of English Language." *God, I'm on fire tonight!*

I could see Mrs Stella thinking this through, and actually agreeing with me. It wasn't her fault she was traditional and stuck to traditional methods. Still, she couldn't let it show, so she offered me a tight smile and said "Just be sure to return back to routine after the Christmas break." I hoped I hadn't burnt my bridges with her. I doubted it. I'd always thought that she may be draconian and scary, but she was fair.

The Christmas exercise was great for me too, as I managed to discover more about my students through reading their pen-pal letters. Dimitra enjoyed Christmas with her extended family—maternal aunt and uncle, their wives, husbands, children and her paternal grandparents. Konstantinos, by comparison, lived in a single-parent household with only his mother and sister, his parents having divorced when he was very young; his writing reflected how protective he was of his sister and mother.

"My mother has to work all the day to afford to send me to the private English school where Miss Rachel teaches, she's from England. My sister she is hoping to go to the University and this also costs money. My mother buy us the clothes, so we don't get many presents, but my sister helps her cook the chicken for Christmas dinner." I began to realise that in order to understand these kids I was going to need to look at their parents and family backgrounds more closely. Only then will the jigsaw fall into place.

Driving home with Manos that evening, I brought up my discovery.

"Yep, Konstantinos's mother is still talked about in the local supermarket and cafés. They usually make reference to Konstantinos's behaviour and say it's not just adolescence; they blame his mother for the lack of a father figure in his life. It doesn't matter about the reality of a situation regarding divorce in Greece," he went on. "The problem, especially in the villages, is that you're expected to stay together regardless, and divorce is a big stigma here. The woman is usually held to blame, for not being strong enough to keep her family together and her man happy."

"That's like the Dark Ages, and bloody appalling in this day and age!" I was feeling more and more protective towards Konstantinos the more I learnt.

"Yes I agree," shrugged Manos, "but mentality takes time to change, especially up here in the villages."

Still feeling quite indignant and more than a little defensive towards Konstantinos, I started to read the pre-teen class's letters at home that evening, eager to see what information I could glean about their backgrounds. By contrast these letters were quite upbeat—or beat-up, to quote Kaliopi—describing the Greek religious practises they observed Most Orthodox Greeks followed the tradition of abstaining from all meat and dairy products, including fish, from 15th November until 24th December.

They then had a big meal on 25th December that included most of the products they'd abstained from, a breaking of the fast, with presents opened on 1st January, the Feast of Aghios Vasilis (Saint Basil).

I had planned to visit Athens the weekend before Christmas…it was also the weekend I was due to fly home. *It'll be good to go clothes shopping, get some more warm gear. And I can't wait to see Dad again.*

Two good things happened on the last day of term: Mrs Stella called me into her office to present me with a cash "Christmas bonus." She made it clear that all teachers received the same: "This is from the government, the equivalent of an extra month's salary." *Ah, not some personal 'gift' or bribe then. Great timing for my spending spree in Athens!* Secondly, my students had gifts for me. The younger ones had drawn a Christmas poster depicting how they imagined a typical snowy English country scene to look.

"Look Miss," Bettina proudly announced, "there is a little house and a snowman and a…umm, *this* in the air"

"Sleigh, Bettina, it's called a sleigh." I smiled at the crude depiction; they'd used cotton wool and tin foil in an attempt to make it realistic. The teenagers had clubbed together and bought me a white woolly hat. Konstantinos, Dimitra, and Litza came forward at the beginning of the last lesson to present it, artfully wrapped in newspaper. I was touched ... and glad to see that the three of them seemed to be getting along.

"You always are saying you have no warm clothes, so this will keep the heat in your head."

"Thank you everyone, *efharisto* and *kala christouyenna*" I attempted the Greek for "thank you" and "Happy Christmas" to wild applause from the group.

"Litza," I pulled her to one side once the class had ended and everybody had said their goodbyes. "Are things okay now among the three of you?"

"Oh yes, Miss. I remembered your Triangle of Love story and didn't want any part of something that sounds so confusing. Besides, Konstantinos has a funny eye, haven't you noticed? It looks to his nose."

I hadn't. I smiled at Litza's observation, wished her a good holiday, and off she went.

"Kala Christouyenna!" everybody shouted to each other. Even the other teachers embraced me, kissing me on each cheek.

After the festivities and high spirits at school, I spent the evening packing bags.

It would be colder back at home; luckily I'd got warm enough clothes there. Packing my cotton t-shirts to the bottom of the drawer, I made a mental note to bring back some winter clothes with me, and there'd be no harm in buying a few new pieces in Athens.

I said *Kala Christouyenna* to Mrs Stella and her husband.

"Ah Miss. Rachel. Here are some *melomakarona* for you to take home." This oval shaped Christmas biscuit was made from honey and walnuts, and tasted absolutely delicious. I wondered if Mr Ioannis had rustled these up, or whether Mrs Stella had exercised a hidden talent. I didn't like to ask. "My sister makes them, you met her once." Mrs Stella answered my unasked question. *Ah yes, the spitting lady.* I remembered her well.

"Thanks—they're delicious."

"They are a Greek Christmas traditional sweet snack. Be sure to save some for your father." *I doubt they'll even last the journey to Athens,* I thought.

After locking the flat's door, I gave the neighbour's ginger cat a friendly pat and made my way downhill to the bus stop. There was the old man, sitting outside his shop and once again, gesturing for me to join him for tea and honey. Alas, I didn't have time—again—but yelled *"Kala Christouyenna!"* He offered a toothy smile and waved, pleased I'd attempted some Greek, and started walking towards me so I moved quickly, wanting to avoid another of his bear hugs. Smiling I pointed to my watch and indicated my need to be quick in order to catch the bus.

As the bus pulled away, I mumbled a "goodbye" to the village, promising to return in the New Year. I noticed the same conductor with the exceptionally long fingernail I'd encountered the previous month. I gave him my small change, surreptitiously looking at his nail for proof of nose picking, as Kaliopi had maintained. *Nope, nothing there to see.* I settled back to enjoy the journey.

When I arrived in Athens, I made my way to Kaliopi's flat, pausing to look at the Christmas decorations. One change to the city that was hard to ignore was damage to stores and shops across the capital, especially in its centre. This was done as a reaction to the shooting of a fifteen-year-old boy, Alexandros Grigoropoulos, on December 6th, by two policemen in Exarchia. Evidence of the week-long rioting, looting, burning of shops, and widespread anger that followed was everywhere: shops with smashed windows were now boarded up, anti-police graffiti was scrawled over many buildings and the Christmas tree in Syntagma Square had been burnt down. The details of the incident were unclear to me, but I'd heard students at school mention it and had been warned by Mrs Stella to steer clear of any conversation related to it—especially with the teenage students. They had mentioned the incident briefly to me, and Konstantinos had asked if I agreed that "all police were pigs."

"I don't have enough evidence to properly comment, and it's always better to know the whole story before expressing an opinion," the diplomat in me had replied. This resulted in a brief moment of disruption from the class whilst they goaded me for an opinion— but I was mindful to try to remain tactful, therefore refused to become dragged in to any heated discussions.

As it was, I still didn't understand what had happened and suspected that the full truth would never be known. All I knew was that an altercation had erupted between some teens and the police in Exarchia, where Kaliopi and her friends had taken me on various occasions. In the scuffle, a young boy had been shot and killed. The week-long rampage and damage that had followed the incident had also been blamed on the ever worsening economic crisis and rising youth unemployment, as well as on government corruption and nepotism.

The evidence of this tragedy really saddened

me. *Athens is a beautiful city, and Greek people are so misunderstood.* I wondered if the Greeks felt the only way to be heard was though revolutionary-style tactics. I was still mulling this over when I rang Kaliopi's bell. Opening the door, Kaliopi announced we'd go to Ermou Street, "for shopping."

We walked along in companionable silence for a while, and then I tried to start a conversation about what had occurred that fateful December day. Kaliopi, however, wouldn't hear of it. She seemed to be in denial and brushed my questions aside with a sweep of her hand.

"I do not want to talk about such things," she stated firmly. "I have had enough of such goings on in my country. And trust me, it will only get worse, these riots. People will mark the anniversary of this boy's death with yet more rioting. So let us go and buy your warm clothes instead. You like H&M, no? It is that cheap shop you also have in the UK. There is one down Ermou also, come." Extracting yet another cigarette, frowning and shaking her lighter, head and hand turned away from the slight breeze in order to light her cancer stick, Kaliopi then proceeded to give me a brief history of the name 'Ermou.'

"In any Greek town where there is an *Ermou Street*, this will always contain shops." She replaced her lighter in her bag, blew a puff of smoke in my vague direction and took me by the arm. "The name *Ermou* comes from *Hermes*, a Greek god who was famous for speed and good luck—but not only; he served as a messenger to Zeus and was the patron of travellers and merchants, amongst others."

Evidence of the rioting was not so obvious once we reached the shopping street, although the street's banks and some of its shops had been targeted for "representing capitalism" and there was a lot of graffiti sprayed over their walls. "Burn the banks, burn capitalism" was a popular slogan, strangely written in English. Most shop owners, however, had managed to get themselves up and running pretty quickly. They'd removed any sign of graffiti and had their glass fronts replaced. I dreaded to think how much their insurance premium would be next year.

I bought a couple more polo necks and a jumper from H&M—it really did get cold in the village—while Kaliopi cured my twinge of guilt about buying non-Greek products by suggesting that we eat at a popular Greek restaurant.

"*Tzitzikas ki o Mermikas*'...'The Ant and the Grasshopper' is the English translation of this place" Kaliopi informed me as we squeezed ourselves into an upstairs table. The restaurant was busy with Greeks and tourists.

The chicken mastic sounds good, I thought, and it was. Chicken pieces atop a nest of pastry, covered with cream and mastic sauce: a natural resin found only in the mastic trees of the island of Chios. We also shared a pomegranate salad—iceberg lettuce, cucumber, and pine nuts, with a balsamic, olive oil, and pomegranate seed dressing.

It was the best food I'd tasted in a long time.

"This isn't the best place to come for food, it's an expensive tourist trap," Kaliopi piped up, almost reading my mind.

"But there are Greeks eating here too. And you

said we'd go to a traditional Greek restaurant" I pointed out as an afterthought. I didn't really mind. The chicken dish combined with the salad was delicious.

"Yes, probably Greek tourists from the villages." I didn't want to get Kaliopi started off again on one of her rants about the Greek villages, so I allowed her the last word: "I didn't say the food was bad here; I said it wasn't the best."

We decided for dessert we'd be even more traditional, so went for *baklava* in Kaliopi's neighbourhood.

"I'll say goodbye and *xronia polla* to you now," she stated later in the evening over take-away pizza. "I'll not be able to come with you to the airport tomorrow—but you know how to get there, no?"

"Yes, I do, no." I smiled at her, confusing my friend with my mis-use of the language.

Early the next morning, Kaliopi once again brewed me a cup of her infamous Greek coffee to drink before my flight home. And as before, I tiptoed out onto her balcony to pour it into her long suffering aloe-vera plant while she was otherwise occupied in the shower. Having said our goodbyes the previous evening I slipped out, leaving Kaliopi a thank you note on the kitchen table. I made my way on the metro to Athens International, feeling excited at the prospect of seeing Dad again, yet strangely a little sad to be leaving Greece, even though I knew I'd be returning in the New Year.

Chapter 10

Arriving at Heathrow was a strong contrast with arriving at Athens International three months earlier. Had I really been away for such a short time? For starters, the weather was decidedly colder. A layer of snow covered the ground. I smiled as Dad embraced me as I exited Customs.

"It's bloody freezing," he stated. "You're looking well and you've lost some weight!" Naturally this pleased me no end, especially in light of all the *baklava* and gyros I'd been consuming. It must have been the daily trudges up the hill. I'm no Kaliopi, with her six kilometres a day runs, but at least the mountain air and Greek lifestyle seemed to be doing me some good.

Dad also looked well. He'd fattened out somewhat, which was a good thing as he was tall and tended to look gaunt if he wasn't careful.

"And you've got fatter," I remarked as we bundled ourselves into the car, ready for the three-hour ride back to the West Country.

"I've discovered cooking!" he exclaimed. "You're in for a treat this visit—I have lots of recipes in mind for us. And as I know you'll probably be missing Greece, I intend to try Mediterranean dishes, too."

"I appreciate it, Dad, but I've been away for a

while, so I fancy English dishes like a good old roast—even beans on toast, or Marmite if possible."

Looking mildly put out, he ventured "Can I at least try out the spinach pie dish I've read about, Rachel?"

"I'm sure it'll taste delicious."

We enjoyed a quiet Christmas together, eating my Dad's attempts at Greek cuisine and excellent traditional English roasts. But the dark evenings and cold, grey days soon had me yearning for Greece again.

"So, Greece seems to really agree with you," it was four p.m. and the curtains had been drawn against the gloomy skies since two o'clock.

"Yes," I brightened...I'd been visibly miserable for the past few hours because of the weather.

"Was I right? Has your dromomania settled down?" I'd looked up this phrase after Dad had first mentioned that he suspected I suffered from it.

"I'm not sure, but I know one thing: there *is* something about the place that makes me look forward to going back and maybe staying a while. And the weather helps, when it is warm."

"Well, in Greece you can do many things deemed illegal in most other European nations," he snorted. "There's a type of anarchy that appeals to the inner anarchist in us all. I knew you'd like it there. And your inability to put your finger on exactly why you like it? That's called contentment, love. Once you finally attain it, it defies explanation...it naturally becomes a part of you. Don't spend too much time analysing it, just accept it."

I loved these chats with Dad. We could spend days simply being together, going to the cinema or watching inane quiz shows on TV, not needing to speak much. Or we could put the world to rights.

Grateful for his insight, I hugged him goodnight. "I still have to pack for the journey back tomorrow, and need to get some sleep."

"Don't forget the teabags and Robinson's Orange squash," he called over his shoulder.

Although the village was still cold in January, at least it wasn't subject to England's floor-to-ceiling greyness. Occasional white fluffy clouds drifted across the blue sky, otherwise most days were cloudless. I could see the snow at the peak of Mount Parnassos as my bus pulled into my adopted home, reminding me of my first arrival.

The village itself hadn't escaped the snowfall either. Dumping my bags, I decided to go wandering, and ended up in the area that Kaliopi and I frequented. Glancing around at the café, I could see snow on the ground and on the leaves of trees that overhung the river, gushing now with snowmelt. The café was closed and Kaliopi was still in her father's village for Christmas. It was January 3rd and she wasn't due to start back at the bank until the 7th. School also started then. The sixth was Epiphany and I was looking forward to this celebration, having heard about the tradition of young men jumping into freezing cold waters to retrieve the crucifix thrown in.

I rose early as Epiphany dawned and wandered down to the river. Although the snow had melted, colder weather had produced ice and I half skidded, half ambled my way down the hill. Mr Ioannis, in his role of Assistant Town Mayor, was already there greeting everybody by the river with enthusiastic handshakes, like a B list Hollywood movie star.

"Where's Mrs Stella?" I asked when he reached me, pumping my hand like a beer tap.

"Bed," he replied, all twinkly eyed. "She no like religious celebrations. But you stay a little, our religion says this day Jesus was baptized. Watch." Aside from asking me if I liked cheese, this was the most Mr Ioannis had ever said to me. I was impressed with his attempt at English and smiled.

At the sound of excitement coming from the river I turned to see the local priest throwing in a large cross. Three virile young men, clad only in bathing trunks, immediately plunged in, vying to be the one to retrieve it. You wouldn't get teens in the UK following tradition and braving ice cold water at nine in the morning. They might do something stupid if they were drunk on the weekend religion of alcohol consumption, but this was different and I was impressed!

A loud cheer from the crowd signalled that one of the boys had succeeded in retrieving the cross. He was lifted onto several shoulders and paraded around, wrapped in a towel and revelling in his success. The atmosphere was proud, happy even, and I soaked it in, watching Mr Ioannis work the crowd, making people feel special—shaking hands, touching elbows of parents and heads of children...*almost like Jesus himself!* I couldn't help observing.

Feeling cold and seeing the café was still not yet open, I made my way home to start planning lessons for the next day. I was looking forward to going back and seeing what my students had been up to. That was a first for me: looking forward to going back to work.

I received a lovely red rose from one of my younger students the next day in class. "You are beautiful, Miss Rachel," she proclaimed, solemnly presenting me with the flower.

"Thank you *agapi mou*, [my love]. Christina, please can you put this in some water?" Christina was the long-suffering school secretary who made the place tick. She could be trusted implicitly and was always being called upon (more accurately, shouted at) by Mrs Stella. My classroom was next to Christina's small office—which was more of a converted cupboard. I'd often hear Mrs Stella's dulcet tones demanding the girl bring something to her office or classroom. I'd never understand what as it was always shouted in Greek, but she'd be expected to drop everything—even phone calls—and attend to the matriarch's whims.

I popped off to do some photocopying in between classes. Christina had provided me with a vase and was dealing with a telephone call.

"What are you doing?" Mrs Stella made me jump, having sneaked up behind me. "Christina will do that, this is one of the reasons I pay her."

"But she's on the telephone, Mrs Stella."

"I don't care. *Christina*! Get here this instant and help Miss Rachel, will you?" she yelled in English for a change...probably for my benefit, but it just made me feel really embarrassed.

I cringed and pulled a 'sorry' face as a harassed Christina appeared in the photocopying room. "I'm sorry…" I whispered, "I was trying to help out by doing it myself."

"Is OK," Christina had long ago resigned herself to Mrs Stella's demanding ways. "Go back to classroom now, before she come back!" We shared a giggle.

My younger classes were brimming with news about their Christmas—the presents they'd received, what they'd eaten, the church services attended. The Konstantinos/Dimitra/Litza soap opera hadn't changed much. Although friends, Litza appeared to display less of an interest in Konstantinos. Their class trooped in at five p.m. for the last lesson of the day and plopped themselves down. Konstantinos remembered he had to sit in the front, chattering away in Greek. When he saw me, he asked, "Miss! Did you have a good Christmas in England?" and seemed mightily pleased with himself for his linguistic efforts. *He's learning to drop the definite article.* I smiled, "Yes, thank you Konstantinos. It was nice to see my father again." But I caught myself and blushed, remembering he *had* no father. This seemed to have slipped by unnoticed though.

"My sister has a boyfriend and doesn't want to help my mother much in the kitchen," Konstantinos started. "And I do not like this boy," he continued. "He is a little *malakas*. I am sorry, but is."

For the first time since Litza had mentioned it, I noticed his right eye. It did indeed have a slight laziness to it. I smiled as I recalled Litza's observation before the Christmas break, and also at Konstantinos's description of his sister's new boyfriend. Still, I had to reprimand him for his language: "Konstantinos! I know it's the first day back but please remember we do not use language like that in this classroom. And besides, no man will be good enough for your sister in your eyes. This is the way things usually go in families—the brother tends to be very protective."

"OK, *Kyria*, but I still don't like him."

The lesson continued without much preamble, everyone keen to get home. At eight p.m. Manos popped his head round the door of my classroom.

"You ready for a lift?"

"OK," I placed my pencil onto the desk and stretched. "Only if you promise to stop at the *spanako pita* roadside café on the way—I'm starving."

As he drove, Manos filled me in on his own Christmas, interrupted only by the stop at our usual roadside jaunt.

"The little one kept us awake all night on Christmas Eve, running into the room, jumping on the bed, bouncing up and down and asking where Santa was. The older one was dead chuffed with his new karate outfit. We ate a lot, went to church on Christmas Day, that sort of thing. You?"

"Just a quiet one with my Dad. It was good to be home, but I'm realising that the weather makes a *huge* difference. It was miserable back in England, and if I'm honest I'm glad to be back. I can cope with cold, but not the oppressive grey."

"Ah, you're one of those *sad* people," observed Manos. "We're lucky. Never suffered from that, being raised in Oz and then coming straight to Greece. Never had the pleasure of experiencing this greyness you mention, not for extended periods of time at least." I'd never given much thought to SAD before, but now he mentioned it...I thought about how weather shapes cultures and habits: it was true that the Greeks seemed to be a hell of a lot more open than their UK counterparts. We British are reserved, ingratiatingly polite, and border on being patronizing when compared to the Greeks and their way of dealing with things.

I remembered my conversation with Dad over Christmas when he'd talked about the anarchical nature of the Greeks. He said something interesting: "The Greeks—well, they're just 'blah' aren't they?"

Yes, they are just 'blah': they say exactly what they think the moment they think it, without processing or refining anything beforehand. And oddly, I didn't get offended by their 'blah-ness'—I actually found it rather endearing and refreshing; I knew where I stood.

Talking of 'blah-ness,' I was looking forward to catching up with Kaliopi the next day, and was the first to arrive at our usual café haunt.

Standing up to embrace her as she jogged up 10 minutes late, she flopped into a chair and immediately lit up her trademark cigarette.

"Back here, again. This year is the year for change. I must get out of this hole from hell," she looked around her. "Anyway, enough about our collective problem that is this place, how was your father and Christmas?"

I filled her in, feeling strangely comforted by Kaliopi's trademark disgust and moaning about her current living and work situation. It felt good to be back, it felt familiar.

Chapter 11

"Ah, Miss Rachel," Mrs Stella cornered me at school one mid-January evening during a break. "I have had a phone call from the local examining board, asking if any of my teachers are interested in becoming oral examiners for the May exam season. I told them that you are a native teacher and that you will be. You will go to Athens this Sunday and attend their one-day training course," she concluded.

Eh? What's an Oral Examiner? And why does Mrs Stella automatically assume I would want to become one?

"Oh, er, thanks." I realised Mrs Stella's opinion that I was worthy of becoming an Oral Examiner was probably a compliment.

"Good, now off you go back to class and I will give you the details later." She gave me a not very gentle shove in the direction of my classroom and swept back into her own. I smiled as I acknowledged that, despite warming to her, Mrs Stella still needed to be in charge. *And she wouldn't look out of place with a cape draped round her shoulders and a pointy hat. Maybe I should buy red patent buckle shoes.*

"What's an Oral Examiner?" I figured the teens would know, so I asked my next class with Konstantinos, Litza and Dimitra.

"Oh Miss," they became visibly excited. "That's really good. You get to examine the speaking part of our exams. This is great—you can tell us what's going to be in the exam!"

Part of the seniors' English examination process was testing in listening, reading, writing and speaking skills. So, it would seem I had been selected to be trained as the Speaking/Oral examiner. "No, I can't tell you that, but I can give you ideas, and be in a better position to help you study in class and look at relevant topics." I watched their faces as they processed this information: that the English *Kyria* wasn't going to tell them outright what to expect, but get them to do some thinking for themselves.

"Just think how much better you'll feel, knowing you've passed an exam due to your own ideas, vocabulary and imagination!" I tried again. Nope—their faces still looked at me like I was stupid.

"I'll give you twenty Euros if you'll tell us what's on the exam," offered Dimitra, lightly tapping her pen on the table, her head inclined as if ready to bargain.

"No! Have I taught you *nothing* about ethics?"

"Well, how about fifty then?" this from Konstantinos.

I took in the sea of expectant faces with growing despair, but also some amusement. I realised these kids had been brought up in a society that believed that everybody and everything had a price.

"Clearly I still have some work to do with you regarding morals. I cannot be bought—you should know this by now. You'll feel so much better passing this exam through your own skill and hard work, trust me. I promise, though, that I will give you an idea of what topics you can expect to cover, for which you'll need a wide vocabulary."

Later, on the drive home, Manos and I continued to discuss the training.

"It's quite a compliment that she's put you down for this, since it's only your first year, and you've not even been teaching a full year yet," he mused. "They like native teachers to do the examining; they've got greater clarity with words. I'm also an examiner, being half Australian and all."

"Well, you have questionable speaking skills yourself," I goaded, smiling.

"Hey, watch it otherwise no *spanakopita* for you tonight," he lightly whacked me on the head.

"Only *tyropita* I'm afraid." We'd stopped the car at our usual spot and Manos passed me the paper with pie inside. "It's a delicious feta cheese pie, good for a change, otherwise you'll end up looking like Popeye." Manos winked as we continued the drive back to the village.

That Sunday I took the early bus to get to Athens in time for the start of the training session. I'd thought about going the night before and staying with Kaliopi, but decided instead to enjoy a day to myself. Besides, she'd tried to discourage me throughout the week:

"My ex is coming to visit again this weekend," she'd casually mentioned during one of our visits to the café.

"Not the Italian with the yacht?" I had images of him trying to throw her off the balcony, given her last experience.

"Eh? *Ochi*, not him. This one's French."

Truly the international, my friend.

"Well you'd better change your bed sheets then," I gave her a knowing smile, she reciprocated with mock surprise and blew smoke in my face.

I arrived in Athens at nine, allowing myself enough time to metro hop to the training venue. Emerging onto a main thoroughfare in the Centre I stood scratching my head, baffled at the Orthodox Church towering in front of me. Looking at my map, I could see this was the right place, but surely we weren't going to have an Oral Examiners' training seminar in a church? *Oh, wait a minute—what's this? I should've realised by now, Athens is full of twists and turns.* There, tucked away behind it stood a smallish building in a tiny alleyway with a crude sign stuck to the church's wall: "Oral Exam training, this way."

I trod carefully down a narrow stairwell, settled down in the basement lecture theatre, and glanced around. My watch read 09:28, but only four people were present. We were supposed to start at 09:30. *Oh well, maybe it's going to be a small session. That'll be good—I can expect almost one-to-one attention.* This turned out not to be the case as Doris, the trainer, clarified.

"Hi everyone," her accent had a slight American twang. "As we all know, this is Greece, so I doubt we'll actually get started until about 10:00–10:15, especially since I'm expecting at least another sixteen of you. You might as well go get a coffee." Not wanting to be so terribly British and the one to point out that it took me two hours to get here and I'd really like to get started, I was relieved when a very large Greek lady chewing gum did this for me:

"Eh, you think we want to stay here all the day, wasting our Sunday? If the others they cannot to get here on the time, then tough on them. Let's get started now. The sooner this rubbish is over, the sooner I can go home."

Well, we'll call you Godzilla from now on, and you're an Oral Examiner with that level of English? I glanced at Doris, waiting for her reaction…but it seemed this affable trainer was either Greek-American, or had been in the country long enough to not get offended any more. She smiled good-naturedly as she agreed and proceeded to hand out the day's schedule and training booklet.

People came in dribs and drabs and by the time 5:30pm rolled around, I was ready to return home. I felt exhausted, my mind buzzing with all the new information. I had to remember to "keep to the script" so as to be fair to all candidates. As a first-timer, all my examinations would be recorded to ensure consistency. I had to be strict with my time limits, making sure I gave enough talking time to students being examined, whilst at the same time paying attention to what they were saying: their grammar, vocabulary, and relevance. I learnt that my students may need some knowledge of the economic crisis, and to be able to discuss in depth their current and future plans.

Blimey, I watched the apartment blocks of the city melt into open fields, *I don't know if I even fully under-*

stand the economic crisis. How can I expect my teens to?

Doris had been very cheerful and supportive, despite Godzilla's continued deep sighs, eye rolling, and huffs and puffs throughout the day. The woman was a teacher at a *Frontesterion* on the island of Evia, approximately two hours from Athens and near enough to the mainland to be connected by a bridge, so she'd driven to the training session. Despite wanting to get started on time, it was also Godzilla who wanted frequent cigarette breaks.

"Maybe we'll finish a little earlier if we skip the next break and work through?" I ventured at one point, only to be stared down intensely enough for me to add a mumbled "But of course, we don't have to."

As we rounded a bend in the road and the view of Parnassos signalled the impending arrival into the village, I picked up my things from the aisle seat—yes, it appeared I was slowly adopting Greek habits—and let out a loud yawn. Today, I'd learnt how to be an Oral Examiner, picked up some important tips for my students and gained yet another comical insight into the Greek psyche. Not a bad day in all. The bus lumbered to a stop outside the *kafineo*, and there was Kaliopi, sitting on the bench, puffing away on a cigarette and scanning the passengers for my face.

"There you are! I've come out to meet the last two buses, in case you were on them."

"I thought you didn't come back from Athens until Monday morning?"

"Yes, but the ex never showed at my place, so I didn't get any sex this weekend," she offered by way of explanation.

"And so you thought you'd come back early and seek out my company?"

"This hole of shit is known for its meat. I know you've had gryos in Athens before, but eat this—it will be better than anything you've had in the past. At least this place is good for something" Kaliopi led me to a different café by the river, pointedly ignoring my remark. "Now, how was this oral day?"

Munching on the *gryos*, which didn't taste any different to me (I kept that to myself) I told Kaliopi about what I had to do as an Oral Examiner. Her eyes glazed over again, so I mentioned the Godzilla lady. This perked her up.

"I bet she was constantly chewing gum like a masturbating cow," she said.

I choked on a piece of meat, smiled, and corrected her. "It's *masticating*—to chew like a cow," I grinned. "You've got sex on the brain."

Ignoring me, Kaliopi continued, "These people who live in island villages—they have no class. Does she think she can examine with a mouth full of gum?"

I was reminded of my first day in class, back in September with the teens. "Well, I need to make the 'no-gum' rule clear to my kids too," I said. "I manage to get them to remove it before class, but they'll also need to remember to do so before the exam. They're always moaning to me because they say it helps them concentrate."

After finishing our food, Kaliopi wanted to go to a bar, despite the fact it was nearly ten p.m. "No," I stated firmly. "You're the one who starts work at 8:30 tomorrow. I don't start until two and can sleep in, but

I'm knackered! It's no fun going up to Athens and back in a day, and having to sit through training."

"Stop moaning, you English person" Kaliopi nudged me in the ribs (a little too hard). "But go on, I understand. You are tired and must sleep. I will see you soon." We parted ways at the bottom of my hill, with a *kali nikta* and kiss on both cheeks.

Spring

Chapter 12

January morphed into February, meaning I could start looking forward to Easter. Unlike the UK, Greece didn't have half-term breaks, and despite enjoying working with the kids and never suffering a dull day, I was becoming worn down and looking forward to the two-week-long Easter break. Manos had told me that Greek Orthodox Easter follows the Julian calendar, whereas Catholic and Protestant Easter follows the Gregorian one. "So Greek Easter, therefore, falls on the first Sunday after the first full moon of the vernal equinox." I wasn't entirely sure what that meant, but basically Greek Easter isn't at the same time as in the UK.

"Look love, I've decided. I might not have long left on this earth, so I'd like to come back to the country I call my second home and pay you a visit." I'd been on the phone to Dad earlier in the week. It was good that he was coming to visit me, but I wish he hadn't thrown so much doom and gloom in there too! Mrs Stella had suggested I go to the local (and only) hotel in the village and book him a room.

"Tell the man at reception you are a colleague of Mrs Stella and you will get a discount. He can't stay with you in your place, it's too small," she said. I bit my tongue in order not to voice my inner thoughts: *So you do recognise that it could do with a little more furniture and decoration then?* I'd seen the local hotel from the outside—and if I could just get rid of the Eagles' *Hotel California* in my head, I'd go and check it out as soon as possible.

"Book my flight for me, using that internet thing," my father decided, and after I got him a good deal, I emailed Stamatis, letting him know Dad would be visiting. I groaned when I read the reply:

"Give me Yianni's flight details, I'll collect him from the airport and drive him to your village." *I hope he finds the drive long enough to catch up with his "dear old friend" and doesn't want to hang out with us all through Easter.* I didn't want to begrudge Dad the opportunity to meet his old friend, but I felt rather proprietorial towards him, and besides, I didn't trust that Stamatis's version of catching up with "my good friend Yianni" didn't involve some strip club full of Eastern European hookers. There weren't any here in the village, but he might take him out in Athens to one.

"Oh, but I will be in my village!" exclaimed Kaliopi when I told her about Dad's impending visit. "Can't you come there?"

"No, sorry. I've made arrangements for us to visit Meteora." We were discussing our Easter plans over coffee one evening. Kaliopi reacted in her usual excitable way by bouncing on her chair when she heard my father was visiting.

"That area is beautiful, not even *I* have been there. The monasteries, those rock formations! It's a UNESCO World Heritage Site. Did you know that a James Bond movie was filmed there some years ago?"

"Yeah, I think it was *For Your Eyes Only.*" I was looking forward to going. I also felt somewhat relieved that Dad wouldn't get to meet Kaliopi. I loved my friend dearly, but I'd no guarantee that in her wide-eyed innocence and penchant for openness, she wouldn't tell Dad an inappropriate tale about a recent sexual exploit.

I popped into the hotel on the main village thoroughfare and spoke to the manager, mentioning Mrs Stella by name.

"Ah yes, I know her husband well. We can do you a discount rate of 60 Euros per night, including breakfast. Come, I'll show you a room." We went up to the first floor and I was shown an en-suite room with double bed. *Pretty small for 60 Euros, and that's with a discount. The view is of the main street, but what choice do I have? And besides, he's not going to be living in here.* I thanked the man and reserved the dates.

I waited anxiously by the phone on Thursday evening. Dad was due to arrive anytime soon and the next day was Good Friday. We'd started and finished the school day earlier because the children's state school had already broken up, meaning we didn't have to teach in the evening. I went back to the "Hotel California" to ensure his reservation was OK, and tidied my small place up... not that *that* took long.

Finally the phone rang. I jumped on it: "Yes?"

"Where's your bloody father?" boomed Stamatis's agitated voice. I sighed inwardly. I'd repeatedly reminded Dad to bring his UK mobile phone and remember to switch it on, and that yes, it *would* work in Greece. Stamatis had clearly tried to call 'his good friend Yanni,' to no avail.

"His plane's landed, I've checked. And I refuse to park my car and pay airport parking fees. So I told him I will be waiting in my 4x4 outside in the waiting bay in Arrivals, and to l*eave his phone on!*"

"It's OK, Stamatis," I placated him. "Give him a few minutes—he might still be waiting for his luggage."

Just before Stamatis hung up, I heard him yell, "Eh, Yianni! There you are, you bloody fool. I have been waiting here for over one hour. Where the hell were you? Did you not listen to me…?" *Thank God for that,* although I felt mildly sorry for Dad since he'd have to endure a car ride with his old friend huffing and puffing. *And what a welcome after more than fifteen years of not seeing one another.* I smiled as I replaced the handset and went upstairs to inform Mrs Stella. Her sister had prepared some meat and salad for us, which I brought down and stored in my small fridge. At 12:30a.m. I received a call from Stamatis again. "We're in front of that bloody hotel. Come and get us, will you?"

I ran down the hill in my excitement to see Dad again. I hugged him hard and made the effort to do the same to Stamatis, noticing that he was *still* giving me the eye! I glanced over at Dad, who seemed not to notice; he was taking in the surroundings, albeit in the dark.

"This is where you'll be staying, Dad," I pointed to the hotel. "Let's dump your bags and then we can walk up the hill to my place to eat. Stamatis," I turned to him, struggling to maintain a neutral expression, "won't you join us?"

"No way!" he exclaimed. "Look at that place, it looks like a shithole! Yianni, why do you insist on staying in shitholes when you come to my country? And you" he turned his attention to me, "take after your *patera*, obviously intent on coming to shithole places—just like your father." I wondered if he was related to Kaliopi. They both think this place is crap and are happy to vocalise it.

Dad and I exchanged a look, but he smiled and clapped his excitable old friend on the back. "Ah, it's just good to see you again, Stamatis old man."

After another round of embracing, back-clapping and making arrangements for when we arrived in Athens, Stamatis finally drove off. We wandered to the hotel to dump Dad's bags and headed up the hill to my place.

"Was the journey OK?" I asked. I was puffing from the exertion of the hill and trying to keep up with Dad—he was obviously fitter than I was at approximately two paces ahead of me.

"Ah, Stamatis is a typical Greek I suppose, he spent the first fifteen minutes bellowing at me for not leaving my phone switched on, getting angry and hitting the steering wheel, telling me he feels responsible for me and was worried you'd be angry with him. I just let him get it off his chest. Afterwards he was fine."

I was itching to point out that in my opinion, Stamatis was an exaggerated version of a "typical Greek." But clearly Dad was pleased to see him again, so I kept quiet.

"Anyway, this place you're staying in is a little sparse isn't it?" Dad puffed slightly as he entered my flat—*maybe he's not so fit after all.* "I mean, it's a good size, but it could do with a sofa or something to make it a bit homier," he looked around, trying to find somewhere to sit. I pulled a plastic garden chair from the kitchen.

"I know, I know, but don't say anything when you meet my boss, I have to work with her. And at least it's warm in the winter and cool in the summer. Plus we've got some great snacks…she figured you'd be hungry."

We spent an hour catching up and eating the food, then Dad meandered back down the hill to the hotel. We planned to spend Easter in the village before heading off to Meteora. Even Kaliopi had advised me to stay in the village during Easter because of its way of celebrating, with lots of meat. "Oh the meat!" she'd exclaimed. "You will find that on Easter Sunday, everyone has stopped being depressed because their Christ has risen again and the skies are black with smoke from the outdoor fires used for roasting the lamb on the spit." It was the first time she'd ever said anything nice about the village.

Despite arriving late the night before, Dad was up by eight the next morning. "There's a lovely river here, with a statute of a woman's head in it!" he exclaimed when I met him at Reception at 10am.

"You've discovered where I go for coffee, Dad. It's a beautiful area, you're right. And that woman's head is the nymph Herkyna, or 'Krya.' I go there a lot to drink coffee with Kaliopi. How did you sleep?"

"Well, the bed's pretty soft, but I did my back exercises this morning, so that helped."

"Morning, John." An Englishman strode through Reception, greeting Dad with a clap on the back.

"Oh hi, I hope everything goes well for you today," Dad called as the man exited the hotel via the revolving doors.

"What happens to him today?" I asked as we made our own way in the April sunshine along the main street back to my place. Checking to make sure the man wasn't within earshot, Dad explained.

"His ex-wife's Greek; he claims she's crazy so he wants to get custody of his little girl. But she comes from a big family, so he has to battle the family in court. He's stuck here over the Easter period, allowed access to his daughter for a few hours each day, and he'll stay until the custody battle is over."

"And he just volunteered this info to you?"

"Well, yes, he sat down at my table at breakfast and just opened up. Maybe it was nice for him to have someone English to speak to. It sounds quite messy and dramatic to me."

"Yes, welcome to Greece," I replied as we arrived at the flat and puffed our way upstairs to make the introductions to Mrs Stella.

The door was opened, just as I muttered "Now *please* be appropriate Dad, she's my boss, OK?" Dad shot me an 'Am I anything but?' look as Mrs Stella shook his hand and led him to the sofa.

"Your daughter is constantly referring to you, Mr John. It is a pleasure to finally meet the man himself." Mr Ioannis, meanwhile, seemed eager to chat about football. The combination of his limited English and Dad's lack of Greek didn't seem to matter one bit as he smiled widely when Dad exclaimed, "Liverpool!" This seemed to start off some sort of weirdly-understood conversation about the sport. Mr Ioannis, it turned out, loved Manchester United, so I left them to it.

"We don't eat meat until Easter Sunday, it's the

tradition" Mrs Stella told us. "I've booked a table for later this evening in a local *taverna*. We'll go to church, light a candle and "feel sad," she dismissed this sentiment away with a wave of the hand. I remembered Mr Ioannis's comments back on the Epiphany day in January: "You know she doesn't like religious celebrations."

"We don't usually attend church," admitted Mrs Stella in a lull in the conversation between the two men, confirming what I already knew, "but tonight we will make an exception, so as to accompany you and be hospitable." She seemed to expect some kind of gratitude. Dad must have picked up on this too: "That's really very kind of you, thank you. We'll look forward to it."

"Can we go back to that river area?" Dad asked. We were left to our own devices for the afternoon.

"She's quite distant, your boss, unusual for a Greek woman," Dad was tilting his head, cat-like, into the sunlight as he sipped on a Greek frappé.

"I know, it took me a while to get used to her, but she's actually very fair in the work environment."

"So long as you're happy love," he reached over to give my hand a squeeze, "and you certainly seem happy." We headed back, needing a siesta.

At eight o'clock we walked further up the hill to the church, accompanied by Mrs Stella, Mr Ioannis and their two teenage daughters—home from Athens for the holidays. Melina, the youngest, pushed her way through the throng outside the church to get us all a small candle.

Having lit one, she then allowed us to light our candle from hers.

"Look at all the people here! Do they usually all turn up to church every week?" Dad asked.

"Ochi!" snorted Mr Ioannis.

"This is a social occasion for people. Look at everyone gathered in their finest dress, chatting to their neighbour. Would you like to go inside?" Mrs Stella asked in her stilted manner.

"Er, to be honest, no," I didn't blame Dad, in view of the crowds of people. We listened to the drone of the priest's voice through the loudspeaker, the mournful sound that reminded everyone to feel very sad today. The crowd started moving in the procession of the bier where the epitaph was carried out of the church and back down the hill towards the town. It was culmination of a day of great 'sadness.'

"Come, we can join them," Mrs Stella instructed. Clutching our candles, we joined the throng. "There's something magical about seeing all these people come together and walking with candles," Dad was taken in. Looking around, I could see people chatting away, appearing not as sad as they should be. "As you said, it's like a social gathering—a time for people to catch up."

Mr Ioannis didn't go unnoticed by the crowd, and part of his duty as Assistant Town Mayor was to be sociable to everyone. It took us roughly forty-five minutes to walk the short distance from the church as Mr Ioannis weaved his magic and chatted to men, mildly flirted with women and clucked at babies and children alike.

We left the crowd at the bottom of the hill to continue on to the town square, whilst our small party turned in the opposite direction toward the *taverna*.

"Best to get there early, before these crowds do. It will get busy once they finish in the square." Mrs

Stella turned out to be correct—the *taverna* was already straining at the seams when we reached it. No ordering was necessary as a set Easter menu had been prepared in advance. We settled down to a simple meal of calamari, bread, and salad. "No meat with blood is allowed, but calamari is OK," Melina explained, sitting next to Dad. It felt a little like being with a pop star as Mr Ioannis back-slapped several people. I noticed Mrs Stella roll her eyes and smile tight-lipped at Dad, who had also picked up on Mr Ioannis's behaviour.

"She's a bit scary, your boss. Pleasant, but scary," Dad whispered. I nudged him in the ribs to shut up, but Mrs Stella seemed preoccupied talking with her youngest daughter, Anthi, about her new hairstyle.

"My daughter has had her hair cut much too short." Mrs Stella turned to me. "Don't you agree Rachel? These young people, Mr Hail, they never listen to their parents" she concluded with another eye roll. Dad and I refused to be drawn into this family battle.

"You see? She can't even be nice to her own daughter!" Dad exclaimed whilst I covered up a snort of laughter as a cough on a calamari piece.

"You'll drink a glass of wine won't you Rachel?" Mrs Stella started pouring.

"Why not? It's Easter after all. And besides, a glass a day is supposed to be good for you. I'd read somewhere it helps ward off breast cancer." *And it's probably better for me than the copious amount of Coca-Cola I drink.*

"Huh—Mum'll be alright then, she gets through a bottle a day," Anthi chimed in. An uneasy silence fell on the table as Mrs Stella's look to her oldest daughter spoke volumes. I breathed a sigh of relief when Mr Ioannis came back...his easy-going nature was infectious. They were so different. I wonder how their marriage works.

By one a.m. Dad and I had gone out separate ways to bed. We'd agreed to meet by the river the next morning.

Chapter 13

"Bumped into that man again at breakfast, he's off to spend a couple of hours with his daughter today." Dad and I were sitting in the late morning sunshine, drinking a frappé and camomile tea.

"Not a lot seems to happen on Easter Saturday," I looked around me. Of course, nothing could keep people from their pilgrimages to the coffee shops or the *Kafeneos*. We'd been warned by both Mrs Stella and the pleasant but portly man at the Hotel reception desk that pretty much everything shut down in the village on Easter Saturday. We'd been invited to Mrs Stella's house for a meal, but not until midnight.

"Why do we have to eat so late?" Dad asked.

"I think people start celebrations for Easter Sunday late the night before," I licked frappé froth from my upper lip, "because they've been fasting and abstaining from meat. Tomorrow is going to be a big day for them with roast lamb and all, so they have to line their stomachs tonight. Oh Jesus!" I suddenly remembered, "you're a vegetarian, what will you *do*?"

"I can make allowances; don't worry," Dad grinned.

"Are you sure? When was the last time you ate meat?"

"Don't you worry about me," Dad reassured me.

We made our way to the café that prepared home-made *moussaka* daily at the bottom of my street. At least this was open today and we intended to buy two big pieces so we wouldn't starve before midnight.

After another afternoon siesta, Dad arrived at my flat at six o'clock, gently nudging the next-door neighbour's cats aside as he entered. We tucked into our re-heated *mousakka* and washed it down with a cup of Tetley. I turned on the TV and the weather girl greeted her audience in her usual outfit (or lack thereof).

"She's supposed to be attractive Dad, is she?" Dad merely snorted with laughter, indicating that he'd never seen anything so ridiculous in his life.

"I've never seen anything so ridiculous in my life!" he confirmed, "and I'm still a man with blood pumping through his veins."

"Okaaaaay, enough of that I think." I switched off the TV, mentally shaking away the images. "Let's head into town."

"The number of times I've navigated this hill of yours in the last couple of days, I'll be super fit." We'd returned about eleven p.m., and after freshening up, we went back to Mrs Stella's house.

"Sit, sit," she flapped as she bustled us to the dining table in the middle of the room. Already perched in a chair was an old lady—Mr Ioannis's mother, and Vasiliki, who stood to envelop me in her arms and shake Dad's hand.

"Watch she doesn't spit at you," I whispered, lifting my chin slightly in the direction of Vasiliki.

"Oh, but that's a compliment, love." I regarded Dad

quizzically. "It means they think you're beautiful, and want to ward off the 'evil eye' or jealousy from others. So they do something negative, like spit at you, which turns out to be a compliment. You're obviously worthy of jealousy from others." I remembered my arrival into the village though; *so that's why Vasiliki had greeted me like that!* And I'd been worried about cleanliness...

"And you know this because...you were spat at when you came to Greece on business?"

"Oh no, not me. But when you came with me sometimes when you were little, you were always spat at, don't you remember?" *Er, no...obviously not.* Dad smiled as I pulled an incredulous face as I digested this piece of information.

"That's disgusting! So I've been subjected to Greek spittle since I was a kid?"

"Yes, but like I say, it's a compliment. Now come on, let's not be rude—come and sit at the table."

Once everyone had sat down, Mr Ioannis's mother launched a barrage of questions that seemed like the Spanish Inquisition at Dad, who was of a similar age to the old woman. The most prominent one concerned his age and how he kept so young looking and healthy. Mrs Stella scrambled to translate.

"You see? He's the same age as you, and yet how different you look," Mrs Stella observed, rather cruelly I thought. "You need to make the effort to get some exercise, Mama." Mrs Stella didn't bother to translate this remark into Greek and actually, 'Mama' didn't understand a word of English and seemed quite content, sitting there gazing at my Dad, occasionally reaching out to pat his hand. *She'd better not spit at him.*

Out came the food. *What was that floating in a clear liquid?* It looked like a long squiggle of colon! I jokingly observed this out loud as I decided to at least try it. "It probably is," Mrs Stella stated nonchalantly. "Let me see? Ah yes, this is *magiritsa*, made from lamb offal. We eat it now to break our fast, after forty days of not eating meat. Tomorrow everyone will be eating lamb on the spit, we need to gently prepare our stomachs tonight for this."

I stopped mid-slurp, shot Dad a horrified look, but he in turn was dealing with his own feelings about this, especially as he claimed to be a vegetarian. We both tried hard to not look disgusted and ate as much as we could. It actually didn't taste too bad—like a watery chicken soup—but knowing what it was didn't help and I just couldn't bring myself to finish it, especially when I was sure I saw an eyeball, but elected not to check if it was my over-active imagination, for fear it might not be.

"This has been a great experience, thank you." We politely made our excuses and left. We were looking forward to the next day's festivities, and besides, Mrs Ioannis Senior seemed to have taken a rather exhausting shine to Dad and kept trying to force more soup his way.

I awoke to the acrid smell of something burning, jumped out of bed, and raced to the kitchen. Nothing was on fire in there. I opened the shutters and understood—the skies were black with smoke from countless barbeque fires that had been lit to roast lamb on spits.

"So, Kaliopi hadn't been exaggerating when she

told me the skies turn black," I opened the door to let Dad in.

"It's like London during the Blitz!" he exclaimed.

"You've settled rather quickly into the Greek habit of exaggeration."

In the small patch of garden by my infamous orange trees, the family had set up their own spit, and Mr Ioannis was busy poking a long metal rod through a whole lamb. I turned away—I'd expected a kebab shop style skewer, not the whole animal.

"For God's sake, you can even see the poor creature's eyelashes," I whispered.

"Well, one thing's for sure—the Greeks know how to prepare meat properly. They don't mess about and become all 'precious' about the issue," he responded. "And they don't waste meat either. Look at what was used last night—the whole lamb's being eaten."

By midday the meat was cooked and then slowly sliced. We all took a small plateful, as well as Greek salad, and sat around munching and chatting. Mr Ioannis and

Dad seemed to be engaged in yet another discussion about football. Villagers passing by would drop in for a small plateful of food as well. When we took our leave later on for a walk through the town, we discovered this was the norm.

"*Ela*, come here, eat, eat!" yelled the man from the oil shop. He was coming towards us with determination, and this time managed to drag my father and me into his back yard where we made our introductions to his wife and older daughter. I was once again spat at, this time by the older lady, but I took it well. Dad barely managed not to laugh.

"I am Evdoxia," the daughter extended her hand. Luckily she didn't spit at me. "My father is always talking about the new English teacher up the hill. It is a pleasure to finally meet you." She lowered her voice to a whisper. "Please, do not be alarmed at my father's insistence on you joining him to drink tea, he gets lonely in his shop all day." It was nice to meet this man's family finally, and we spent a pleasant hour eating his lamb and nodding along to the conversation, Evdoxia translating occasionally.

"Dad, I don't think I can stomach too much more—as hospitable as everyone is, I'm going to burst. Let's have our siesta now and I'll see you later." We'd not managed to make it to the river…at least two other people who I vaguely recognised as the supermarket check-out lady and the baker had pulled us into their gardens for yet more lamb. It didn't seem to matter that we weren't close friends or relatives; such was the hospitable nature of these village people.

There was another church service that evening. This time the cry from the loudspeakers was much more cheerful—today was a celebration. But Dad and I decided not to attend, we had a train to catch early the next morning, to Meteora.

Chapter 14

"Shall we just take a taxi?"

"OK," I agreed. "It's too cold at this time of morning anyway." We were standing by the bus stop in town, waiting for the shuttle to take us to the train station. Having observed the quaintness of this rural train station before, I'd become blasé about it, but it was a first for Dad.

"Look at this place." He looked around him as the taxi dropped us off. "It reminds me of the countryside stations when I was evacuated as a kid." At this early hour, the only other noises came from the man behind the ticket counter, who was chatting on his mobile phone. There were no other passengers on the platform; they'd probably all left earlier in the week so as not to have to travel on Easter Monday. Any passenger traffic would come later in the day—people returning to start work the next day. Luckily, working for a school meant I had the whole week off.

Leaving Dad on the platform, I went to purchase the tickets. The station master seemed to be deliberately ignoring me, 'busy' with his phone call. It wasn't until I exclaimed very loudly *"signomi"* [*Excuse me*] that he turned to me with a bored expression. I decided to treat us both to first class.

"And we have a whole compartment to ourselves! This really is like the old-fashioned trains," Dad continued his admiration of the Greek rail experience once the train squeaked to a halt and we boarded.

"And you wouldn't believe how much the tickets were, Dad...only twenty-five Euros each, first class." I decided not to share the experience with the station master with Dad, not wanting to tarnish his ideal of the journey so far. I marvelled that the journey would take us about three hours, and compared that to the price of a three-hour journey in first class on a UK train. There was no comparison, really.

We settled into our seats, closed the sliding outer door to our carriage and gazed as the train cut through mountains and sped past shepherds' huts, the occasional shepherd tending to his sheep, arm raised in greeting as our train snaked past him. There were decidedly fewer lambs in the fields. I guess they'd all been eaten by now.

"There's hardly anyone on this train," Dad returned from the buffet area with a Styrofoam cup of coffee. "For a state-run enterprise, I'd say these trains are better maintained and cheaper than the privatized ones back at home."

"Well, privatized or not, one thing doesn't seem to change—the toilets," I'd just had the privilege of visiting one. Yes, suffice to say that Greek and British toilets on trains remained equally disgusting; irrespective of the fact we were the only ones using them in First Class.

I fell into a doze, just as the train slowed to approach Kalampaka, where we were due to get off. Peering out, I glimpsed great monoliths—the Meteora pinnacles. They looked ethereal, especially with banks of low clouds shrouding the summits.

Arriving at the guesthouse, my Dad once again tested the firmness of his bed.

"At least my back won't hurt too much. This mattress is much better than the one in the village hotel." We were sharing a twin room, something I hadn't done since I was a child. I hoped his snoring hadn't worsened over the years, and congratulated myself on the fact I'd packed earplugs, just in case.

"I might have to lob a sock at you in the night if your snoring's worsened."

"*Me snore?* Ha! We'll see about that." I didn't have the heart to remind Dad that one of the cited reasons in the divorce of my mum and Dad, for unreasonable behaviour, was 'snoring so much at night so as to inhibit basic daily functioning due to excessive tiredness." *Maybe if Mum'd worn ear plugs...oh well, no point in going down that route now.*

Having tested the bed and unpacked, we made our way into the town. We were surrounded by the ancient, towering rock pinnacles, which managed to look both majestic and eerie.

"It's beyond comprehension that they were created over sixty million years ago." I was struggling to get my head around it.

"It says here they were sculpted by wind and earthquakes," Dad read from a local guidebook. "Yes, they are indeed amazing."

After a simple lunch in a *taverna* in the town square we decided to explore further. The guesthouse was set amongst some of the rocks and a path cut its way through them. Scattered around were the small houses of Kalampaka, and before long we came across a small Orthodox church.

"I don't think this is one of the monasteries," I said. It wasn't; those were perched atop the rocks themselves. More than twenty had been originally constructed, dating back to the fourteenth century. However, only six remained today—four inhabited by monks and two by nuns.

"We'll visit the monasteries tomorrow," I said as we made our way back to the guesthouse, a little yapping dog following us most of the way. He'd appeared from behind the church to play. We stopped to play for a while…he looked like a little spaniel and was quite happy to roll onto his back to have his belly rubbed.

We fell into bed, exhausted from the day's travel and looking forward to visiting the monasteries the next day.

Mum hadn't been exaggerating when she cited Dad's snoring in the divorce. I'd stopped myself at one point last night from chucking one of Dad's slippers at him, the noise was so loud. *Don't forget, you're glad he's here* I kept repeating as I lay there, earplugs firmly planted in my inner ear. I finally managed to sleep about two am.

"You snore too loudly," I couldn't help myself grumbling as we bundled into the taxi. We'd negotiated a good price with Nikos, a local taxi driver to drive us up to, and around, the six monasteries. A trek by foot from the guesthouse to the top of the rocks would've been strenuous, plus it was drizzling. Besides, I was too tired from lack of sleep.

"I love you too, sweetheart" Dad said. I smiled, despite myself. In the warmth of Nikos's Mercedes cab, we rode up and arrived at the first, the Holy Monastery of Varlaam.

"It's the second-largest monastery, inhabited by monks," Nikos told us. Leaving him at the base, smoking a cigarette out the taxi window, we scrambled up the staircase cut into the rock to reach the entrance. Access to these monasteries was originally made very difficult due to fear of occupation, requiring either long ladders or nets to haul people and goods up the sides. Finally in the seventeenth century, staircases were cut into the rocks. "Good job too," remarked Dad. "You wouldn't get me sitting in a net to be hauled up, not with my back."

We gazed around in silence at this great place, built in 1541. Neither of us had any words as we looked out over the great courtyard to the sweeping views of the fertile plains of Thessaly below. There was no sign of any monks, however.

Next stop was the Holy Monastery of St. Stephen, which sat atop a flat plain, not one of the ancient rocks. Fewer than ten nuns lived here. We went up to pay our entry fee, and an elderly nun pointed to my trousers, then a sign that proclaimed "Women must wear skirts to cover their legs" in various languages.

"But my legs are covered" I stated, reasonably I thought, until Dad nudged me hard in the ribs and smiled benignly at another nun who was handing me a sarong.

"I am afraid all the women must where the skirts and not the trousers. It is offensive for women to dress as men. Please wrap this around your jeans," she smiled.

The nun looked about the same age as me, if not younger.

"So, if I came in wearing a miniskirt, I'd be allowed entry, but not in trousers?" I was determined to get to the bottom of this warped logic. I could see Dad covering up his embarrassment.

"No," replied the nun patiently. "They must also cover the legs with these items," she indicated the basket of skirts. "They must just not to wear the trousers, it is too manly." I tried to probe further, it just didn't make sense. "Why...?" I started. But Dad was gently but firmly pulling me along, nodding at the growing queue of Greek tourists behind them.

"Sometimes, love, you have to just accept religious and cultural differences and stop asking 'why.' You wonder why you used to constantly get detentions at school? Well, your desire to question teachers all the time got too much! Come on, let's accept, let go and enjoy this place." I grudgingly backed down as I wrapped the awful piece of sarong material around my waist. It just about brushed my ankles and upon spying a brown stain at the front, I stopped myself from trying to imagine how many other people had worn this before me.

Peering over the edge of the courtyard, we stood in awed silence yet again and gazed at the rope ladder that spilt over the edge from a small hole in the monastery's wall, another example of how people used to get supplies up to the place. "I wonder if anyone's fallen trying to get up to these places." Dad's question echoed my thoughts exactly.

Our third stop with Nikos was the Monastery of the Holy Trinity, inhabited by monks and used in the 1981 James Bond movie "For Your Eyes Only." By the time ve came out, Dad had decided he was all monasteried out for the day. Besides, the weather had deteriorated from a light drizzle to a steady rain.

"*Malakias (bullshit)*" Nikos swore under his breath. As we were driving back, we rounded a corner, only to be confronted by a goat herd and his shepherd. Dad and I didn't mind having to slow down, it was a great photo opportunity. Nikos had his window open and one or two goats stuck their heads in, making Nikos swear even more.

Finally we arrived back at the guesthouse for a shower, change of clothes and last meal in Kalampaka before heading to Athens the next day. Dad would spend the night with Stamatis, me with Kaliopi, before Dad flew back to the UK and Kaliopi and I returned to the village.

Chapter 15

Lying in bed one Friday morning, I reflected how—only three weeks earlier—Dad had been with me and we'd experienced the delights of a Greek Easter and the Greek countryside. He'd arrived back in the UK safely, after a night with Stamatis doing God only knows what—*there're some things a daughter is best not knowing about her parents.* Embracing me hard at the airport, he'd then held me at arm's length:

"You look fantastic, love. This country is doing you some good. It's not just the food, I see a change in you, a sort of mellowing. See? I *told* you Greece grabs you and takes you in." I waved a slightly tearful goodbye to him, looking down at myself and realising that yes, I had had to make another notch in my jeans belt to tighten it. I'd lived off spanakopita and gyros, which probably accounts for my weight loss.

Kaliopi was most disappointed she'd missed Dad, and insisted on hearing all about Meteora. "Hypocrites, that's what those nuns are," she stated when I told her my skirt story. "They are men-haters, that's why they're nuns---don't want women to wear trousers because they look like men—huh!"

"Actually, Kaliopi, I thought they were really gentle and calm people, and I'm not religious in any

„hape or form." I felt the need to stick up for the kind woman who'd patiently insisted on my wearing a skirt and equally patiently explained why.

"Huh—listen to yourself: one visit to a nun place and you're ready to convert!" Kaliopi blew smoke into myface in mock disgust.

"No worries there, Kaliopi, I'd get vertigo living there and besides, you'd never come and visit me," I re-assured her.

"Of course not—and besides, they wouldn't let me in once they see how many male visitor 'friends' I have. They wouldn't want me corrupting you."

As May came around, it grew warmer. The snow at the peak of Mount Parnassos started to melt and the Oral Exams crept up. My students had become increasingly agitated in class—especially the 'Terrible Threesome:' Konstantinos, Litza and Dimitra. I put this down to exam nerves and tried my best to improve their vocabulary in areas surrounding the economic crisis and its effects, as well as a range of other subjects, such as environmental problems. *The more I read, the more I learned as well! Mrs Stella will be pleased.*

"Miss, what's a word for those people that come into our country and take our jobs, you know—those people from India and stuff?" asked Konstantinos.

I took a deep breath. I had to remind myself that these kids hadn't been exposed to such integration—unlike myself—and Greece and other Southern European countries seemed to be some sort of 'holding area' for illegal immigrants trying to enter Europe. It was a very complex problem—one I suspected Northern Europeans were not keen to see resolved anytime soon as it suited them to keep illegal immigrants out of their own countries...but it didn't help my immediate cause and besides, I wasn't about to get into this debate with Konstantinos and his posse. Contentious as his comment was, at least he was trying.

"I tell you what, Konstantinos," I turned on what I considered to be my most winning smile—"why don't we take a look at how the 'crisis' has affected this immediate area."

Litza started. "Well, my uncle he can't sell potatoes like he used to...he says it's because they must be a certain size for the EU. So he not bring home much money anymore." I even learnt something interesting myself: Apparently the region where the village and school were located was thought to have high concentrations of mercury in the soil, therefore farmers often had problems selling their produce...once every couple of months they would take their vegetables and fruit to Athens and in a united attempt (and to prove there was nothing wrong with their wares), would give it away free in a central market.

"It's all a lie, Miss!" said Konstantinos—he'd started to refer to me in the English form, not the Greek now...he'd dropped the word *Kyria*—"They are trying to make out we are bad people...there is nothing wrong with our food! Look at me." I smiled at him.

"Indeed, look at you!" I replied, not unkindly. "And the word you were looking for was 'migrant', Konstantinos: people who go to a country other than their own to find work. Greece has a long history of migrating…look at how many Greeks are in Australia and the U.S., for example." I was determined to give him food for thought.

Manos collected me early morning on the last Sunday in May, and off we went to examine in a town about an hour away.

"Jump out here," he pulled up at a three story school building in the centre of the rather ugly town, "I'll go and find somewhere to park." We'd passed a long snaking queue of nervous looking teenagers outside the building—all waiting their turn to take the exam and for once, most had arrived early, vying to be the first in.

Announcing our arrival at the Reception of the grey Communist-style building, we made our way upstairs to collect our 'packs.' Kept strictly under lock and key, it wouldn't have been out of place to label them 'Top Secret' as they contained the topics and questions for the Oral Exam.

"You must *not* leave your room unattended with this inside," instructed the unsmiling, severe looking woman as she passed our packs over and we signed them out, "a student could, and probably will, find his or her way in and arm his or herself in advance with knowledge."

Manos and I gave our most sincere and serious nods in affirmation, whilst I smiled to myself; this was something I could imagine Konstantinos trying to do, and probably succeeding in.

We examined in pairs: one person asking the questions and the other sitting, listening to the students' replies and allocating the marks. Luckily I was paired with Manos, as I'd spied 'Godzilla.'

"What's wrong with you?" he asked as I tried to make myself inconspicuous behind him. "Come on, let's go to the room. You wanna question first? Half way through, we'll swap to give your vocal chords a break—trust me, they're gonna need it!"

Our examining room turned out to be the school gym with a table and chairs set in the corner.

"Whey hey, look at *this*," Manos walked towards a huge chess set, the pieces sitting at waist height. "Oh, and *these*," he further noted as he ran childlike to the set of ropes hanging from the ceiling and tried to scale them, all the while making monkey noises.

"Manos!" I hissed, "The first candidates are sitting outside and can probably hear us, let's sit down eh?" I was feeling really nervous. Some kid's future in English would partly be decided by me. All their months of study would finish today, so I had quite a big responsibility.

Zoe and Melanthe turned out to be the first "victims."

After going through the rigmarole of getting them to spell their names, I started on the first question:

"So Zoe, what do you like about living in your town?" I offered her a beaming, encouraging smile.

"Nothing," she sulkily replied, arms crossed and eyes looking at the floor. I waited a good five-seconds to allow her to redeem herself, figuring she might be

…ervous.

"OK then, Melanthe, how about you?"

"Oh, I like the sun and I like the drink café with my friends and I like the cinema and I like the television and I like the volleyball and I like the…."

Behind me, Manos interrupted with a loud cough. Taking the hint, I tried to move them along.

"Zoe, I'm going to show you a picture and I'd like you to tell us what you see," *This is like an ink-blot test!* I placed a black-and-white picture of a family seated around a dinner table, the woman dishing up a meal. Zoe took one look at it, laughed, and retorted in perfect English.

"Well, that's just typical, a woman serving the food. I can see a *typical* Greek family [she spat out the word 'typical' as if it had a bad taste] and they are eating *typical* Greek food like *mousakka* and *pastistichio*. And like a *typical* Greek family, the woman is cooking and serving all the men first. The daughter will have to collect the plates and wash them up and…." Again Manos interrupted this rather impressive diatribe from the previously reticent Zoe with a prolonged clearing of the throat.

Rather nervously now, I passed Melanthe's picture to her and she attempted to describe a silly picture of another family, this time in a water park. Privately I wondered if I had wasted my time getting my kids armed with vocabulary about the economic crisis if they were going to be looking at pictures of rather simple scenes. Or maybe that was the Greek way: the exam board tells us to prepare the kids for one thing, only to be tested on something much simpler.

Melanthe's contribution couldn't be more different than Zoe's: "Oh *look* at the happy faces of the young children in this extended family! They all look so happy, going down the water slides and they all want the day not to end and they will go to the home at the end for the big family meal with the grandma and grandpa..." as she said this, Zoe threw her a dirty look and actually, I was sure I detected a hint of sarcasm in Melanthe's otherwise naïve demeanour and definitely caught her throwing a sideways smile at her fellow candidate. *Are they colluding together? Good cop/bad cop?*

Manos's throat-clearing saved the day once again. Eventually the exam wound to an end, and with some relief I noted that the last questions required knowledge of everyday events and economic problems. I was also somewhat relieved that this exam with this particular set of students was drawing to a close. I'd found them exhausting.

"Goodbye!" I beamed as they left the gym. Puffing out my cheeks in a long sigh, I raised a questioning eyebrow to Manos who delivered his opinion.

"That first girl—what's her name, had a bloody chip on her shoulder and the other girl sounded as if she'd inhaled helium! Got to admit though, that first one, Zoe? She picked up when faced with the picture—but I sure wouldn't want to be the man that marries her. At least they both had the vocabulary. I'm passing 'em." Smiling I agreed with him and now, feeling less nervous having got the first candidates out of the way, I felt OK about waving in the next batch.

And so the day progressed. By six pm we'd seen over fourteen pairs of students between us and taken

.urns in examining and marking. I was knackered by the time we came to collect our cash for our day's work.

Driving home, Manos made a quick call to Mrs Stella.

"Our kids are being examined tomorrow," he explained. "I want to let her know the content of the exams so they know what to expect."

I sighed inwardly. Despite my trying to teach the kids to take the moral high ground, it appeared that even my boss was trying to take shortcuts and accept any help she could. If this level of "corruption" was happening from the top, was it any wonder that it went on further down the chain and reached my kids? I pondered the complexity and ramifications of this thought and realised it pervaded Greek society as a whole—even at government level…ha, *especially* at governmental level.

Chapter 16

With the exams out of the way, the end of term was approaching—it would coincide with the end of May. We still had one week of lessons left, but now that the older kids had finished their exams, they were much more relaxed in class.

"Have you ever had a Greek boyfriend, Miss?" Litza and Dimitra asked one day... Konstantinos sniggered in the back row. I was trying to conduct a lesson from the grammar book, but as it was the last week even I didn't have the energy to teach formally. *As long as they're speaking English, at least they're learning something.*

"That's none of your business..." I tried to change the subject, but this went right over their heads. They weren't going to give up this line of questioning.

"It's nearly the end of the lesson." At that moment Christina rang the hand bell to signal the end of class. As the others left the class, I kept the threesome back, "Come on, you promised me coffee once, remember?"

We ambled along to the nearest coffee shop, located by the bus stop. Konstantinos plucked a rose from the garden of one of the school's neighbours and proudly presented it to me.

"I'd love to accept this, Konstantinos, but I'm

rry, you must put that back, it's not yours to give away." I was determined to instil some values into him. He looked genuinely rejected as we sat down, so I allowed him to order and pay for my coffee.

"In answer to your question about whether I've had a boyfriend here in Greece is no, not yet—I've been too busy teaching you!"

"But, Miss, you must have a life, a life of the heart, and that means having a relationship whilst you're here. You cannot leave Greece without meeting a man; it is unheard of!" Konstantinos clearly held views on this.

I sipped my latte and smiled at him, noting how much he'd improved in my time of teaching. Not only in his English. His sulky, reticent attitude had also mellowed: there was no way he'd be seen sitting with his English teacher in the local café at the beginning of the year. I thought about Kaliopi's ability to fall so easily into relationships, even if they were just one-night stands.

"To be honest, I feel as if I have fallen into a relationship—one with your country as a whole. So much so, I'm considering staying here," I thought aloud, "which will give me plenty of time to meet some*one*."

"Oh yes miss, but don't stay here," Dimitra pulled a face, Litza copied her.

"Why not? What's wrong with here?" asked Konstantinos.

"I want to go to the big city and meet a city man," Dimitra looked purposefully at Konstantinos. I remembered Zoe's attitude in the Oral Exams just a few weeks previously, and smiled.

"Don't you want to try life in the city, Konstantinos?" I asked.

"Huh! There's nothing I can get there that I can get here," he stated proudly. "The food is fresher, and besides, who will look after my Mum?" I noted the difference between a seventeen year old Greek boy and a teenager of the same age in the UK: they were desperate to leave home, whereas Konstantinos seemed quite taken with traditional ways. But not Litza and Dimitra; they were both pulling faces and looked as if they couldn't leave this 'hole from hell' fast enough. *Maybe there isn't a future for Dimitra and Konstantinos after all.*

That night, over coffee with Kaliopi, I thought about my conversation with my students and the thought that I might come back. I hadn't realised the idea had even been on my mind until I'd said the words aloud.

"You're not coming back to this shithole," she characteristically claimed. She'd finally mastered the correct usage of the word. "*Look* at this place, and you can't stay another year in that flat. Anyway, I hope to be living in Athens next year—I've requested a transfer and they're actively looking to relocate me back home, thank God," she concluded.

Did I want to stay in Greece? I'd certainly enjoyed my time here, discovered a passion for teaching, and developed a love of a country that holds family values dear to its heart. I didn't come from a close family…but I felt as if I finally belong somewhere. And if I went to Athens next year, I'd have more of a life.

I decided not to return to the UK straight after

ıching. Instead I booked a few days in Santorini to ▪elax and consider the possibility.

"You look like a woman with a lot on her mind," declared a man who looked about fifty, placing an un-asked for cappuccino on the table in front of me and sitting himself uninvited in a chair opposite me.

"Nikos," he introduced himself as he shook my hand. "I doubt there's a better sunset than this in the world. Whatever *malaka* made you come to Santorini alone and look so thoughtful is an asshole. Men these days are just boys; they have no knowledge of how to treat a woman."

After unpacking my belongings in the small guest-house, I'd slowly made my way to the café to watch the sunset over the caldera, and had purposefully chosen the quietest café in order to people-watch and just *be*. I forgot, however, that I was in Greece…and not just Greece, but Santorini—the most romantic island of them all—and I was a single woman. It was beyond the comprehension of many Greek men to see a woman alone. So my thoughts were interrupted by this Nikos character.

I smiled and gestured a thanks for the coffee.

"*Tipota*, nothing," he dismissed. "So what brings you to Santorini alone?" He nodded sagely as I told him, as briefly as I could, my experiences of teaching and how I was thinking of staying in Greece.

"And whilst I may be physically alone, I don't feel it. I feel as if Greece is my family, and she's looking after me. It's the first time I've felt truly accepted in a family, after never really being accepted in my own. bit my tongue as soon as I'd said it… again not realising until I'd said it out loud that that was how I felt. *Greece accepts me, whereas my sister never did. I didn't realise I was so affected by her rejection.*

"Greece does this to people … sucks them in, but in a positive way. Some people aren't able to see beyond the surface beauty of this place," Nikos sighed as he swept his arm towards the setting sun. "Others such as yourself, *copela*, you have experienced the *real* Greeks and their hospitality. What is there to even consider? Go back to your country with the rain, wind and cold and your *malakismeni* sister…or stay here and experience blue skies every day!" He leant forward in his seat, as if he was about to impart some top secret information. "You, *copela*, are an honorary Greek. I see it in your eyes. You've embraced this culture and feel accepted here— *of course* you must stay." Nikos stood up, massaged my shoulder briefly, and gathered up my drained coffee cup. As he reached the entrance to the café, he turned back to me. "Now that we have sorted that out, enjoy your time here. There's no need to waste time thinking … just be." I smiled to myself, remembering that "just being" was the whole purpose of my visit to this café in the first place. "And come back tomorrow evening for watching the sunset—you're welcome here."

I grinned at his pidgin English, biting my tongue to stop myself from automatically correcting him. Yes, I would relax and enjoy my time here. It appeared that I would be staying in Greece after all. *Thanks for sorting that out Nikos.* I couldn't wait to tell Kaliopi.

"So it appears I'm staying." I announced. Kaliopi and I were sitting in our favourite coffee shop in the village. I'd told her about my experience with Nikos on Santorini and was now back in the village, spending the last few days before moving my stuff to Athens and storing it in Kaliopi's flat for the summer while I went home.

"How will your Dad feel? Won't he want you back in the UK?"

"I thought you were all for me staying."

"Of course, but I just wondered."

"We chatted last night." I recounted the conversation. "He said he's seen a change in me; apparently I'm more settled now than when I lived a 'settled' nine-to-five existence. He doesn't want me to live the life I think everyone expects of me…and besides, he wants to come and escape the UK weather once a year."

I grinned as I remembered his words: "Rachel, when have you ever given a toss about convention? And besides, don't think coming back to the UK and getting a desk job will suddenly make your sister approve of you. If she doesn't approve now, she's never going to, regardless of how you live your life. Let go of your angst; you can't choose your family and it seems you have better sisterly relationships with the friends you've made there than you'll ever have from your own flesh and blood."

As usual, he was spot on. I swallowed back tears.

"So where will you work?"

"Mrs Stella's set up an interview for me in Athens with a well-known school owner."

Chapter 17

Waking up at about eight a.m. in Kaliopi's Athens apartment, I noticed she'd already left for her new job. The transfer from the village had been remarkably quick for her. In the kitchen, I read the note she'd left: "Coffee in the pot. Do the washing up please—you'll be helping me out." Scratching my bed hair and yawning loudly, I eyed the pile of dishes in the sink and the left overs of last night's pizza.

Having washed up and dressed in my trademark black trousers and light purple shirt, I sat at the kitchen table counting the bonus pay Mrs Stella had pressed into my hand on my last day

"You have worked hard this year, my dear, and I wanted to thank you," were her parting words. Not used to such a display I tried to protest the extra money, saying it was my job.

"Yes, but it was a job well done, and this is my way of thanking you," she repeated. When I saw Kaliopi, she had backed this up. "Get used to it, it's the Greek way." I'd felt embarrassed and flattered. After all, I had mixed feelings about my boss and had spent time laughing with Manos about her draconian ways. He'd given me the *spanakopita* recipe as a present. Dad would love that. The other teachers had been characteristically remote

...d just wished me well in the staffroom on the last day. *Oh well, they'll have a new member of staff next year.*

Deciding there were worse things in life than receiving an unexpected one hundred and fifty Euros in cash, I made my way across town to the centre of Athens, ready for my interview with the formidable owner of my potential new workplace.

"Yes?" enquired an attractive and well-groomed receptionist, looking up from her computer.

"Yes, hi, I'm here for an interview..." before I could finish my sentence, she barked "Teaching or Editing?"

"Teaching" *Does she have to be so rude? And what does she mean, editing?*

"Wait here," she gestured towards a bench seat whilst she went off into a small room to the right of the reception area. I looked around. There was a TV screen repeating a video of a nativity play. It seemed the younger students here took part in a Christmas play every year.

"She will see you now," the receptionist announced from the doorway. Gesturing that I should go in with a flick of her head, I stood up, smoothed my trousers, adjusted my top and entered the small office.

I needn't have worried—sitting in the corner was a well coiffured elderly brunette who looked me up and down twice and exclaimed, "Well, you've got the job... just go and see my secretary to arrange your timetable."

"Er, don't you want to see my CV and my recommendation letter?" I felt like I was missing something, that I needed to try harder or that it wasn't *possible* to simply land a job just on looks.

"What's there to discuss? You're a teacher and clearly a professional woman." I was subjected to the up and down scrutiny yet again, "so you have a job, starting in September. Do you need somewhere to live? We will arrange all that—now go, I am a busy woman. Go and talk with the secretary." I was waved out of her office. Clearly my time was up and luckily for me, I appeared to have made an impression.

Feeling somewhat bewildered by the experience, I was shown by the fashion model receptionist into yet another side room; to meet another secretary. The place resembled a rabbit warren. A name plague stated she was Mariela and she placed her pen and glasses on top of her pile of paperwork, smiled wearily at me, indicated the seat opposite and again repeated the mantra: "Editing or teaching?"

"Teaching," I informed her. "But what's this editing?" Mariela rubbed her eyes as she explained the nature of work at this particular school.

"We're not only a school; we run our own editing department and write our own teaching materials. So, we employ staff to do both tasks. Do you want to do both tasks?"

"I've never edited before, can I let you know?"

"Sure sure, plenty of time before the new term starts in September. We can discuss then. Now, we will have an apartment ready for you when you come back, the term starts on the 19th but you will need one week's training, so make sure you're here for 10th September. See you then." I backed out of this slightly more affable

.ady's office, thanking her.

Later that evening, Kaliopi and I were drinking coffee near the Acropolis. "The whole process was over in about 10 seconds. They took one look at me and offered me the job! I felt a bit like a prostitute, without the sex bit, obviously." I remembered Stamatis's and Mr Ioannis's once-overs. It wasn't just the men, then.

Watching the tourists wander by, Kaliopi said: "So you were subjected to the Greek scrutiny and made it through. Well done." She took a deep breath. "I have some bad news though: I am leaving for Barcelona in the summer. I have a job offer there—an international branch of our bank," she looked sceptically at me, not knowing how I'd react. I smiled at her.

"Fate's been good to me, Kaliopi. Going into that interview, I hadn't been too sure whether I wanted to stay or not—now it seems it's decided for me, I'm happy. And I'm happy for *you*. You and I saved each other in the village…now things are working out for you. I'll never forget our coffees, or how you introduced me to all things Greek. We'll be friends, regardless of where we are or how often we do or don't see each other." She hugged me, tears welling up in her eyes.

"Come! You're making me cry," she wiped her eyes with the palms of her hands. "Now come home and help me choose my bed sheets. You may be flying back to the UK tomorrow, but Andre is coming over." I grinned: "Just take it easy with the Spanish men—and take plenty of washing powder."

"I thought you'd have got it all out of your system by now. You know, come back and settle down to a proper lifestyle. But you're saying you want to go back?" Kirsty was on a roll again. *No change here then. Really, what did I expect?*

It was déjà vu. The three of us were once again sitting around the kitchen table and I'd told Dad and Kirsty that I'd be returning to Greece for another year. This time, however, I was TEFL qualified, had a job secured in Athens, a good friend in Kaliopi and something else; I was a tougher, more resilient person. I had developed a Greek sense of *den pirazei*—never mind. Let people be who they were, and try not to mind.

"I said a year ago, Greece sucks you in, and besides," my Dad turned to Kirsty, "at least she seems to have found her anchor now, so stop giving her a hard time. Just because it's not your version of a settled life, it doesn't mean it's wrong." He turned back to me and winked. This was the longest speech my Dad had made in support of me, especially in front of Ugly Big Sister. I smiled and straightened my back. Even in my mid-30s and despite my personal growth, I could *still* feel somewhat belittled and undermined by Kirsty—but this time, instead of feeling unsure about my decision, I knew deep down that to return was the right thing to do. So *what* if I led a 'rolling stone' lifestyle; at least it made me an interesting person. I looked over at Kirsty and I felt a rush of affection; *It's not her fault she's so prickly.* I reached out and stroked her hand, smiling at her. *Kaliopi and Greece has taught me a lot about displays of affection.*

Regarding me with suspicion, she snatched her hand back and lent forward in her seat. "Listen," she pointed, "I know all about the economic problems out there, so don't go thinking that by being nice to me, you'll get any money—or my share of Dad's Will money when he dies."

I took a long, hard look at her.

"You really don't like me, do you," it was a statement, not a question.

"I don't like what you represent," she leaned in and whispered.

"And what's that?" I knew I shouldn't be drawn into any sort of confrontation—exactly what she wanted, but I was intrigued.

"Freedom, selfishness, the ability to do what you want."

I realised there and then that it didn't matter what I said or did, she had already made her mind up about me. I sighed. Whereas in the past I would have taken such negativism towards me personally, now I saw her for what she was: a sad and bitter divorcee who lashed out at family because that's what she felt they were there for. *And what kind of person already kills her own Dad off before he's dead?* Any affection I felt previously was snatched back, just as quickly as her hand. Taking a deep breath, I put the tougher, new Greek 'me' into action:

"Listen. Dad's not dead yet, I don't live the same lifestyle as you. I am younger," I paused and added as an afterthought "and prettier, let's face it, but all these facts don't give you any right not to hear me when I speak, not to take me seriously, to look at me like you trod in a piece of shit. Like it or not, I am family—just like I accept you as family. So as long as we see each other, then I want no more barbed comments about my lifestyle choices, right? You can choose to accept it and maybe even come out and visit me one day, or continue the way you are and lose a sister. If you have nothing nice to say to me, do everyone a favour and don't bother opening your mouth." By the end of this monologue, I was trembling. It was the first time I'd ever really stuck up for myself.

Not bothering to wait for a reply, I threw an apologetic look at Dad, *he's going to have to deal with the aftermath,* and took myself off, intending to walk through the fields that surrounded our house. I felt proud. *Siga siga*—slowly slowly as the Greek's say. *My growth is coming slowly.* As I left, I could hear Kirsty's high pitched "Did you hear that? She shouldn't be allowed to talk to me like that, I'm her older *sister*, I'm a *teacher*!" I couldn't resist sticking my head back into the room and retorting, "Try acting like it then!" Dad responded by turning on Radio Four very loudly to listen to the cricket score.

Negotiating a kissing gate to enter the nearest field, I found myself grinning. Stopping to watch a cow and her calf exchange nose rubs, I shouted "I'm free, I'm *Greek*," startling a flock of sparrows from the nearby oak tree. Yes, I was going back 'home', and I couldn't wait.

Thank you for reading my debut novel. Indie authors rely on reviews so if you enjoyed it, do please head to Amazon and/or Goodreads to spread the word!

And feel free to contact me via my website www.lifebeyondbordersblog.com for more adventures in Greece and worldwide.

Ack..

I would like to thank the follown.

Russell Bowers for his initial input—wit.
book would not have developed beyond the .
Scott, founder of *Girl Gone International,* to
for the book title. Tina Jones of *Girl Gone Inter*
for her invaluable editing. Jessica Bell of the *Ho ieric
Writer's Retreat* on the Greek island of Ithaca, and Chuck
Sambuchino of *Writer's Digest* who ran the course at this
retreat. Their ongoing encouragement helped me believe in
myself and get this finished. Natascha Maria for her patience
and arranging the layout for me, it was a big job! A huge
thanks to the extended network of authors I have met online:
Savannah Grace, Sara Alexi, Torre DeRoche, Nene Davis,
Samantha Verant and Sonia Marsh to name but a few—all of
whom have been a tremendous support, especially during the
times when a lack of belief that this book would ever come
to publication took over. Marissa Tejada, fellow expat author,
helped me through the process, and Caroline and Nigel
Daniels became, over time, part of my extended family who
grew to be as excited about this novel as I am! My thanks
to my editor, Perry Iles, for tirelessly working through the
script several times. Then there are the friends and characters
I made in Greece itself, without whom this book would never
have been possible—especially Artemis, I love you, crazy
one! Finally, huge thanks to my father; my anchor, my rock.
And ironically to my siblings; without our relationship, this
book would not have been written.